ECONOMICAL writing

Chicago Guides
to *Writing*, Editing,
and Publishing

ECONOMICAL
writing

THIRD EDITION

Thirty-Five Rules for Clear and Persuasive Prose

Deirdre Nansen McCloskey

With an Appendix by STEPHEN T. ZILIAK

THE UNIVERSITY OF CHICAGO PRESS

Chicago and London

The University of Chicago Press, Chicago 60637
The University of Chicago Press, Ltd., London
© 2019 by Deirdre Nansen McCloskey
Appendix © 2019 by Stephen T. Ziliak

Earlier versions of this book were previously published by
Macmillan (1986) and Waveland Press (1999). Any questions
concerning permissions should be directed to the Permissions
Department at The University of Chicago Press, Chicago, IL.

Published 2019

Printed in the United States of America

28 27 26 25 24 23 22   4 5

ISBN-13: 978-0-226-44807-7 (paper)
ISBN-13: 978-0-226-44810-7 (e-book)
DOI: https://doi.org/10.7208/chicago/9780226448107.001.0001

Library of Congress Cataloging-in-Publication Data

Names: McCloskey, Deirdre N., author. | Ziliak, Stephen Thomas,
    1963–
Title: Economical writing / Deirdre Nansen McCloskey ; with an
    appendix by Stephen T. Ziliak.
Other titles: Chicago guides to writing, editing, and publishing.
Description: Third edition. | Chicago : The University of Chicago
    Press, 2019. | Series: Chicago guides to writing, editing, and
    publishing | Includes bibliographical references and index.
Identifiers: LCCN 2018048196 | ISBN 9780226448077 (pbk. :
    alk. paper) | ISBN 9780226448107 (e-book)
Subjects: LCSH: Economics—Authorship. | English language—
    Composition and exercises. | Academic writing.
Classification: LCC PE1479.E35 M33 2019 | DDC 808.06/633—
    dc23
LC record available at https://lccn.loc.gov/2018048196

∞ This paper meets the requirements of ANSI/NISO Z39.48-1992
(Permanence of Paper).

Contents

Preface

The implied reader of my little book is a student of any age who realizes that in her middle-class occupation she needs to write. And write. And write. Doing the writing better will pay. And anyway, writing well enriches the soul.

The book originated at the University of Chicago in the 1970s in a course for graduate students in economics. An early version, directed at young professors of economics, appeared under the present title in the April 1985 issue of *Economic Inquiry*. And something like the present edition, directed at economists more generally, appeared in book form at Macmillan of New York in 1986 as *The Writing of Economics*. In publishing the first edition Anthony English, then at Macmillan, was tasteful and energetic. Tony was the last editor of the classic little book by Strunk and White, *The Elements of Style*, and it was highly flattering to me to see my own *libellus* in the same form. The present book can be viewed as a follow-up to Strunk and White, more advanced. (That would be flattering too.) In 1999 Waveland Press revived the book with revisions that pushed the implied audience beyond economists. The present book from the University of Chicago Press is in effect a third revised edition, addressed to a still wider array of writers in economics, business, government, the social sciences generally, and history and literature. Let's all do better, economically.

I thank a group of good writers who improved the argument in its earliest form by telling me where it was wrong or right: Eleanor Birch, Thomas Borcherding, Ross Echert,

Clifford Geertz, Albert Hirschman, Sara Hirschman, Linda Kerber, Charles Kindleberger, Meir Kohn, David Landes, much of the McCloskey family (Laura, Helen, and Joanne), Joel Mokyr, Erin Newton, Carol Rowe, much of the Solow family (John, Barbara, and Robert), Richard Sutch, Donald Sutherland, Steven Webb, A. Wick, and Barbara Yerkes. Getting someone to criticize a piece of writing early is a good practice—though writers who put themselves up against a deadline, as most of us do, seldom have time to follow it. It's better to be criticized harshly by friends in private, and fix what's wrong, than to be massacred in public. I've had the benefit. The John Simon Guggenheim Foundation, the National Endowment for the Humanities, the Institute for Advanced Study at Princeton, and the University of Iowa gave me the time for the first and then the second edition. Retired from the University of Illinois at Chicago, I now have *plenty* of time. (Ho, ho.) I have time, for example, to take the excellent advice of Joe Jackson, an editor at the University of Chicago Press when I first contemplated revision, and from Mary Laur, Holly Smith, and Ruth Goring of Chicago at the end.

I added three new chapters (32–34) for this edition, starting with one on standard forms in letters and emails. The new chapter on writing English for nonnative speakers comes from a decade and a half teaching students at the summer academy of EDAMBA, the European Doctoral Association in Management & Business Administration. And the new chapter on how to make a presentation comes from many decades of listening to good and bad presentations.

I include a piece by Rachel Toor in 2016 for the *Chronicle of Higher Education*, in which she interviews me on writing and living. And "House Rules," which are my own teaching materials in using the book.

My coauthor on numerous projects and dear friend Professor Stephen T. Ziliak of Roosevelt University invented many years ago an effective way of using the book, the "McZ♯ method," which he kindly describes in an appendix here. Ziliak aims to get students to become their own best editors, using my chapter numbers to find the flaws in their papers themselves, and to rewrite fixing them. That's what we seek.

You, oh student, can do it yourself, before your teacher or boss gets annoyed by the correctable flaws in your writing.

Why You Should Not Stop Reading Here

The woman in the street loves her erroneous opinions about "fair" trade and will not listen to professors of economics contradicting them. Her opinions are her own, after all, and policy on trade is "just a matter of opinion." Everyone in a free country is entitled to an opinion. Phooey on the professors. But a student of even elementary economics will have read the chapter on comparative advantage in his Ec 1 text, from which he learns that the woman in the street and the man in the White House are embarrassingly ignorant. If you want to learn to think about anything, and stop being embarrassingly ignorant, you should start by listening to experts, as the apprentices do on *This Old House* on the Public Broadcasting System, or as you did to your gymnastics coach.

It's like that with writing. Most writers have at first the amateurish attitude of the woman in the street about policy on foreign trade, and have opinions like the novice carpenter's erroneous idea of how to cut studs for a new ceiling. They don't know the rules and the reasoning behind the rules. They won't look into professional advice on writing. They never rewrite. They won't read the page they wrote yesterday with a cold eye. They admire uncritically everything they've written, favoring their mistakes as God-given and personal. Just matters of opinion.

It's true that you can't change your character traits very much, and it's offensive for some louse to criticize them:

LINUS: What's this?

LUCY: This is something to help you be a better
person next year. . . . This is a list I made up of all
your faults. [Exit]

LINUS [reading, increasingly indignant]: Faults? You
call these faults? These aren't *faults*! These are
character traits!

Amateur writers suppose that writing is a character trait
instead of a correctable skill. If someone says that it's amateurish to use "not only . . . but also" or that it's vacuous to
use "process," they are liable to react the way they react to
remarks about their body shape: Hey, that's who I am. Lay
off, you louse. The professionals, by contrast, such as poets
and journalists and the best writers in business and government and academic life, have learned to take advantage
of criticism — and in the writing itself they take advantage
of their own self-criticism. The first and the biggest truth
about writing is that we all — you, I, and George Will — can
use more criticism of our style of writing. We would be
more professional if we took it more seriously.

1 Writing Is a Trade

In a *Shoe* cartoon strip long ago, the uncle bird comes in the front door with a briefcase overflowing with paper and says to the nephew bird, "I'm exhausted, but I've got to work. I've got to get this report out by tomorrow morning." Next panel: "I'll be up until 3:00 writing it." Last panel, picturing the nephew with a horrified look on his face: "You mean homework is forever?!"

Yes, dear, homework is forever. A lot of it is writing.

Outsiders have been complaining for a long time about how economic and sociological and business and bureaucratic writing gets written (Williamson 1947). I'm an economist by training, a historian by avocation, a professor of English by late-life passion. People in all fields write. Unlike professors of English, though, only a few economists and historians have written about the craft of writing or taught it to their students. As a result, the standard of economic and historical writing has declined steadily. For example, nowadays even pretty good writers of economics and history and, yes, English use locutions like the academic "as we will see," the newspaper version being "more on that later," pointlessly anticipating in a manner you never see in Alfred Marshall (1842–1924) or Lord Acton (1834–1902), or even John Maynard Keynes (1883–1946) or A. J. P. Taylor (1906–90). The economist Walter Salant did his part in an essay published in 1969. In 1978 J. K. Galbraith wrote a piece called "Writing, Typing and Economics." He was referring to the novelist Ernest Hemingway's crack about the Beat Movement novelist Jack Kerouac: "That's not writing: that's typing." A lot of writing in economics, history, business, government service, the military, and on and on isn't even very good typing.

No one tells the beginner in a craft with a lot of writing how important it is to improve it. The researchers at the US Department of Agriculture, surprisingly, do care about writing. It's a tradition in the department. So do some Federal Reserve banks. Private companies do a lot of business by writing, and their CEOs often claim to care how it's done. On the other hand, presentations in business, and now too in academic life, are dominated by the worst of PowerPoint. Academics of course must write, feverishly, if they are to get tenure and the respect of their colleagues. But many of them do so with a trowel. In most colleges the undergraduates are taught nothing about writing after the compulsory first-year course in composition, which they try to forget. The graduate students do not get even that. The master carpenter turns her back on the apprentice, concealing the tricks of the trade, such as how to cut a board without splintering the back of the cut.

The big secret is that good writing pays well and bad writing pays badly. Rotten writing causes more papers and reports to fail than do rotten statistics or rotten research. You have to be read to be listened to. Bad writing is not read, even by professors or bosses paid to read it. Can you imagine actually *reading* the worst report or term paper you've ever written? Your sainted mother herself wouldn't.

A couple of trowel-writing professors of economics attacked the article version of the present book by claiming that actually obscurity pays off. Well, suppose it does.

Suppose I'm wrong that bad writing pays badly. So what? Being bad is bad. The sainted mother I mentioned told you to be good, period. Being clear — or, to use the term of art, "readable" — is an ethical matter beyond mere profit-making prudence (McCloskey 1992).

2 Writing Is Thinking

Another reply to instruction such as what's offered here is "That's just a matter of style. After all, only content matters." Students will sometimes complain about bad grades earned for writing badly, arguing that they had the *content* right or that they *meant* to say the *right* thing (people who complain about grades speak in italics). Your boss probably won't tell you outright that she thinks you're an idiot on account of the shocking illiteracy of the last report you turned in. But you'll get the point soon enough, with a pink slip or a lack of promotion. And anyway you want to do a good job, for your personal and professional self-respect. I know you do.

The influence of mere style is greater than you might think. Ideas are not merely "conveyed" or "communicated," as though through the pneumatic tube at the drive-in bank. In communication studies we call "conveying information" the "conduit metaphor," which is not meant as a compliment. Any idea changes, sometimes radically, in its expression and in its reception. The history of ideas has made many wide turns caused by "mere" lucidity and elegance of expression. Galileo's *Dialogo* of 1632 persuaded people that the earth went around the sun, but not merely because it was a Copernican tract (there were others) or because it contained new evidence (though it did). It was persuasive in good part because it was a masterpiece of Italian prose in an era in which most scientific writing was in scholarly Latin. Poincaré's good French and Einstein's good German early in the twentieth century were no small contributors to their influence on mathematics and physics. John Maynard Keynes (rhymes with "brains") hypnotized three generations of economists and politicians with his graceful fluency in English. Keynes is acknowledged as the best writer that economics has had. Yet look at the hostile dissection of the style of a passage from Keynes in Graves and Hodge (1943) 1961 (33–40). It makes one wince that the best is so easy to fault.

You can't split content from style. They constitute yolk and white in a scrambled egg. The conduit theory says that content sits in one brain until it is communicated by pneumatic tube to another, unchanged in the communication. That's true of *sheer* information, like your phone number or the place you left your keys. But it's not true of knowledge. Knowledge relies also on judgments, which you discover and polish in conversation with other people or with yourself. Therefore you don't learn the details of your argument until speaking or writing it out in detail and looking back critically at the result. "Is what I just said foolish. or is what I just wrote a deep truth?" In the speaking or writing you uncover your bad ideas, often embarrassing ones, and good ideas too, sometimes fame-making ones. Thinking requires its expression. You can't add 23 and 27 if you get all fuzzy about whether 3 plus 7 equals 10 or 11. You have to know. Good thinking is accurate, symmetrical, relevant to the thoughts of the audience, concrete yet usefully abstract, concise yet usefully full of good ideas. Above all it is self-critical and honest. So is good writing.

Good writers, that is, write self-critically and honestly,

trying to say what they mean. Sometimes you'll discover in the writing that what looked persuasive when floating vaguely in your mind looks exceptionally foolish when moored to the page. You'll discover, too, truths you didn't know you had. Annie Dillard says in *The Writing Life*, "When you write, you lay out a line of words. The line of words is a miner's pick, a woodcarver's gouge, a surgeon's probe. You wield it, and it digs a path you follow. Soon you find yourself deep in new territory. . . . The writing has changed, in your hands, and in a twinkling, from an expression of your notions to an epistemological tool" (1989, 3).

Writing resembles mathematics. Mathematics is a language, an instrument of communication. But so too language is a mathematics, an instrument of thought.

Rules Can Help, but Bad Rules Hurt

Like mathematics, writing can be learned. You are merely evading the responsibility to overcome your ignorance, such as we all have, if you talk of writing as a natural gift, a free lunch from the gods that some people have and some don't. It's an excuse for not doing your job in a workman-like manner. Although we can't all become Mark Twains or Virginia Woolfs or George Orwells or Annie Dillards, anyone can write better than they used to. In fact, Twain and Orwell, like Dillard, worked at explaining how (Twain 1895; Orwell [1946] 1968), and Woolf's essays are models for any student on how to write.

Elementary writing can be learned like algebra. On the simplest level, neither is inborn. Very few people can prove important new theorems in mathematics or make highly original and important points concerning Shakespeare's *Othello*. They're as rare as people who can write regularly for the *New Yorker* magazine. Yet anyone can learn to solve a set of simultaneous equations or learn basic Shake-spearean definitions (for example, *honest* meant mainly "aristocratic," not truth-telling, a highly relevant point for *Othello*), just as anyone can learn to delete a quarter of the words from a first draft.

Like mathematics or literary criticism at the simplest level, good writing at the simplest level follows learnable rules. Rulebooks on writing, most of them pretty good, proliferate like mushrooms. Read 'em. (By the way, the preinstalled programs in Microsoft Word and the like that claim to help you with writing are useless. Turn them off. They advise you, for example, to put a comma in a sentence after every introductory phrase. In Dutch, yes, a rule. In English, optional, a choice.)

You can find the good rulebooks in the writing section of any big bookstore. My three old favorites, from elementary to advanced, are William Strunk Jr. and E. B. White, *The Elements of Style* (1959 and later editions); Robert Graves and Alan Hodge, *The Reader over Your Shoulder: A Handbook for Writers of English Prose* (1943 and later editions); and Joseph M. Williams, *Style: Lessons in Clarity and Grace* (1981; 12th ed., with Joseph Bizup, 2016). Not everyone will get as much as I did from the three. But Strunk and White is fundamental. You can't be any kind of professional writer if you haven't read and taken to heart its little lessons. "Express parallel ideas in parallel form." I catch myself daily *not* doing it. Then I force myself daily to do so.

Other texts I know and admire come from the era in which I was actively trying to improve my own wretched style by being a student of the masters. (By now I have become The World's Leading Expert, as President Harry Truman expressed it: "An expert is someone who doesn't want to learn anything new, because then he wouldn't be an expert.") Note that all the books think of readin' and writin' as learnable crafts, not inherited genius. A few of the best are Richard A. Lanham, *Revising Prose* (1979; 5th ed. 2007) and his *Revising Business Prose* (5th ed. 2006); and Wayne Booth, Gregory Colomb, and Joseph Williams, *The Craft of Research* (1995; 4th ed., with Joseph Bizup and William T. FitzGerald, 2016). Some more advanced books are F. L. Lucas, *Style* (1955; 3rd ed. 2012); Jacques Barzun, *Simple and Direct: A Rhetoric for Writers* (1976; 4th ed. 2001); part 3 of Jacques Barzun and Henry F. Graff, *The Modern Researcher* (1970; 6th ed. 2003); Paul R. Halmos, pages 19–48 in Norman E. Steenrod et al., *How to Write Mathematics* (1973; 2nd ed. 1981); Sir Ernest Gowers, *The Complete Plain Words* (1962 and subsequent editions); Howard S. Becker, *Writing for Social Scientists* (1986; 2nd ed. 2007); William E. Blundell, *The Art and Craft of Feature Writing* (1988, by a writer for the *Wall Street Journal*); Francis-Noel Thomas and Mark Turner, *Clear and Simple as the Truth: Writing Classic Prose* (1994; 2nd ed. 2011); and anything instructional by Annie Dillard, such as *The Writing Life* (1989), which I just quoted.

But some of the books on style are surprisingly bad, so watch out. A good test is whether you read the book with pleasure. If a so-called master carpenter does not know how to cut a board clean, maybe you better not become his apprentice. (By the way, here's how: nail a piece of scrap to the back of the piece to be sawed, flush with the cutting side. Cut both boards. The scrap piece prevents the saw from making splinters on the other side of the piece to be sawed.)

Many of the rules I give here are the same ones the other books give, but some are my own creations from observing writing by me and by others. They will be depressing at first, because of their great number ("Number 613: Query any sentence with more than two adjectives") and their vagueness ("Be clear"—but, you ask, how?). What you are trying to learn resembles good sewing or carpentry, watching what you're doing and giving it some thought, having learned from others. Long ago I heard a paper at a conference on writing called Writing on the Bias (published as Brodkey 1994). "On the bias" is a term from sewing, cutting and sewing a piece of cloth diagonal to the weave to make the finished skirt swirl gracefully. The author's mother was a brilliant seamstress, and her sewing, said her daughter, taught the daughter how to write, making the prose swirl gracefully. I myself learned how to work at writing from watching my mother tearing down (non-bearing) walls and studying ancient Greek. She finished jobs, such as a brilliant poetic autobiography called *The Strain of Roots*, written slowly, daily, self-critically over thirty years after her husband died. If you resolve right now to put away your amateur attitude toward writing and to start observing and thinking about your own style, you'll do fine. Meanwhile, as with the first steps in sewing or carpentry, learn the rules and rules and more rules.

Don't believe everyone, though, who sets up as a teacher. The first rule here is that many of the rules we learned in Ms. Jones's class in the seventh grade are wrong. Sometimes of course Ms. Jones had a point. For example, dangling out on a limb alone, she justly castigated modifiers badly placed in a sentence. Read a sentence from the *Washington Post* (12/29/2017): "That confusion was echoed among thousands — some following the advice of their accountants — who interrupted their holiday activities to line up at tax offices." It paints a picture of *accountants* lining up, not clients, because of where the "who interrupted . . ." is placed in the sentence. Put the word or clause relevant to X close to X. Thus, from an email I wrote and then revised, "I'm traveling a lot, to Las Vegas in a couple of weeks, for example, a strange place" should be instead "I'm traveling a lot — in a couple of weeks, for example, to Las Vegas, a strange place." If people are going to grasp immediately what's "strange," they need it to be close to "Las Vegas." I'm telling you.

Yet in many ways Ms. Jones's rules and the associated

folk wisdom have done grave damage. "Never repeat the same word or phrase within three lines," said Ms. Jones. The rule fit splendidly our budding verbosity at age thirteen, so we adopted it as the habit of a lifetime. Now we can't mention the "consumer" in one line without an itch to call it the "household" in the next and the "agent" in the next. Our readers slip into a fog known in the writing trade as "elegant variation."

"Never write 'I'," wrote she, and we (and you and I) have drowned in "we" ever since, a "we" less suited to us mere citizens than to kings, editors, and people with tapeworms. "Don't be common. Emulate James Fenimore Cooper. Writing well is writing swell," said she, praising Harry Wimple in the second row for his fancy talk—and in later life we struggled to attain a splendidly dignified bureaucratese. Her strictures against "I" make no sense if they merely result in replacing "I" with "we." But they do make sense if you note that when you're talking about "I" (or "we") you're not talking about the subject. Talk about the subject, class.

Ms. Jones ruled against our urge to freely split infinitives. H. W. Fowler, who in 1926 wrote an amusing book on the unpromising subject of "modern English usage," knew how to handle her ([1926] 1965, article "Split Infinitives"): "Those who neither know nor care [what a split infinitive is] are the vast majority, and are a happy folk, to be envied by most. 'To really understand' comes readier to their lips and pens than 'really to understand'; they see no reason why they should not say it (small blame to them, seeing that reasons are not their critics' strong point)."

Ms. Jones filled us with guilt about using a preposition to end a sentence with. In English you have a choice: "a service **for which** people were willing to pay" or "a service **which** people were willing to pay **for**." Usually getting the preposition out of the final position is better, though it's best to judge by sound, not by rule. The rule you learned in school to *never* leave the preposition at the end is mistaken. Winston Churchill (1874–1965) was a British politician of note who wrote English well. About his very lofty Harrow School he said that the boys learned Latin as a duty and Greek as a treat (the economist Keynes won the Greek composition prize at another such school). Being no good at either, Churchill claimed, he merely learned English astonishingly well. Legend has it (though it might just be legend) that this master of the language wrote in the margin of a manuscript corrected by a student of Ms. Jones and her rule of no prepositions at the end of a sentence, "This is the sort of impertinence up with which I will not put."

Worst of all, Ms. Jones fastened onto our impressionable minds the great and terrible rule of Jonesian Arrangement: "Say what you're going to say; say it; say that you've said it." The person who first formulated such a memorable way of putting it is now being tortured for eternity in hell. (Bertrand Russell, the great British philosopher, is said to have done the foul deed. If he did, shame on him. But he never actually wrote his essays or books according to it.) The rule drains the drama from your writing. It is b-o-ring. Writing that follows the Jones rule — in business, in government, in academic life — therefore consists mostly of summary, outline, anticipation, announcement, redundancy, and review. It takes forever to get to the point, if ever. As British prime minister during the Second World War, Churchill used to require that any proposal to him, no matter how major or minor, be written on a half sheet of paper. The requirement prevented "I am going to say, I say it, I have said it."

4

Be Thou Clear; but Seek Joy, Too

Once you learn a few of the rules and start applying them, you'll start to be able to play the Game of Writing. It's not merely a grim following of rules, a death march to the Department of English. It's fun to get a sentence just right, in the same way that it's fun to get a dish you're cooking just right or get a double play in baseball just right, Tinker to Evers to Chance. The psychologist Mihaly Csikszentmihalyi ("CHICK-sent-mee-high"; we call him Mike) has discovered that happiness is not a six-pack and a sport utility vehicle but what he calls "flow." It occurs "when a person's skills are fully involved in overcoming a challenge that is just about manageable" (Csikszentmihalyi 1997, 30). Flow makes work into play and play into work. The rhetorician Richard Lanham argues that you teach yourself writing by some clowning around. You take words seriously by playing with them, overcoming an artistic challenge that is just about manageable. You do it in your emails to your brother. Bring a similar skillful clowning to your professional writing.

I don't think, in other words, that life should be mainly rule driven. Learn the rules in order to be joyously creative. To have a fulfilled life, you want to achieve flow. Skillful writing is one of the ways.

The one genuine rule, a golden one, is Be Clear. An ancient Roman professor of writing and speaking put it this way: "Therefore one ought to take care to write not merely so that the reader can understand but so that he cannot possibly misunderstand" (Quintilian 8.2.24). Clarity is a social matter, not something to be decided unilaterally by the writer. The reader, like the voter in a democratic country, runs the show. If the reader thinks what you write is unclear, then it is. Quit arguing. Karl Popper (1902–94), an Austrian-origin philosopher with a good English style and a correspondingly wide influence, wrote: "I learned never to defend anything I had written against the accusation that it is not clear enough. If a conscientious reader finds a passage unclear, it has to be re-written. I write, as it were, with somebody constantly looking over my shoulder and constantly pointing out to me passages that are not clear" (Popper 1976, 83).

Clarity is a matter of speed directed at The Point. Bad writing stops you with a puzzle in every other sentence. It sends you as reader off in irrelevant directions. It distracts you from The Point, provoking you to wonder what the subject is now, what the connection might be with the subject a moment ago, and why the words differ. You are always losing your way. Bad writing makes slow reading. The practice of Graves and Hodge in *The Reader over Your Shoulder* was "to glance at every book or paper we found lying about and, whenever our reading pace was checked by some difficulty of expression, to note the cause" (Graves and Hodge (1943) 1961, 127).

In most writing the reader is in trouble more than half the time. You can see it by watching your own troubles. I once sat in an airplane beside a young man who had just graduated in engineering from Iowa State University. We fell into conversation, and he admitted to me as the professor that he was always losing his way in paragraphs. He therefore had given up, assuming that he had some sort of mental deficiency, and had never read an entire book. I tried to persuade him that *everyone* has his "mental deficiency." I'm not sure he took on the point, but it's true. A colleague of mine in history said to me once that the great obstacle to being a scholar is learning to read without falling asleep. That's right. You should as a writer work on keeping the reader awake.

Notice in the present long and involved sentence, because there is a lot of clumsy intrusion of brand new stuff and jumps in elevation of lingo, how no one could follow it, at least on first reading without having to go over it two, three times, maybe four, because it is ungrammatical, which means not only that it breaks a Ms. Jones Rule but also that it confuses you and anyone else, a reader, who happens to be reading, by violating your expectations, and that it has too much in it anyway, with no pleasing arrangement, which would make sense of it. You stumble and wander and fall asleep when you read such stuff.

Reading your own writing cold, a day or a week after drafting it, will show you places where you, the brilliant author, cannot follow with ease even your own sense. That's the Graves and Hodge trick. Knock such places into shape. If the reader has too much trouble, she gives up. Lack of clarity is selfish and confusing. The writer is wasting your time. Up with this you need not put.

For example, as you write you will think of new things to stick in. That's fine: writing is a tool for thinking. Remember Annie Dillard's remark. But when you come to revise, seeking the politeness that is clarity, you will want to rework and rearrange phrases to straighten out the one-more-thing effect. Thus "That it is New York, and you will help me enjoy it (as I always do), is good" should be "It is good that it is New York, and you will help me enjoy it, as I always do."

Telling someone who is not already an accomplished writer to "be clear," though, is not a lot of help. It has been said that "it is as hard to write well as to be good." In the abstract the golden rule of writing helps about as much as the golden rule of other doings, of which it is a corollary. "All things whatsoever ye would that men should do to you, do ye even so to them." Well, sure, yeah, all right. But how?

5 The Rules Are Factual Rather Than Logical

The rules come from observation. In the best writing you don't stumble. It's no trick to spot a bad sentence and to see what went wrong. Just read. You feel it, like rain or sunshine. You know that George Orwell wrote well, that Mary McCarthy doesn't take many false steps, that you seldom have difficulty understanding what Tom Wolfe is talking about. Samuel Johnson said two centuries ago: "He who would acquire a good style should devote his days and nights to the study of Joseph Addison." Well, likewise Orwell, McCarthy, and Wolfe.

You can't define good style without a list of good writers. A list compiled statistically (and somewhat dubiously, I would say) for economics by Arthur Diamond and David Levy (Diamond and Levy 1991, 6) showed that the best writer in economics was, uh, me. It is *extremely* depressing news, for economics and for me, because I know perfectly well how badly I write. To remind me of my incompetence by a standard tougher than writers of economics I only have to open a copy of the *New Yorker* and read more than the cartoons. If I'm the best . . . aaaaach. I much prefer, among the economists who write for newspapers, Paul Krugman, Donald Boudreaux, and Richard Rahn. Of the more private writers, Yeland Yeager and Thomas Schelling and Robert Frank never bore you, if you have a taste for economics. In an older generation Robert Solow and George Stigler and Alexander Gerschenkron were never actually painful to read, and often were funny. In a much older generation in English, Keynes, Robinson, Machlup, Haberler, and Schumpeter would make the list (the native language of the last three was German). And once you get used to his eighteenth-century prose, you will discover that Adam Smith wrote with passion, mixed with a sarcasm that makes some of us LOL.

Good style is what good writers do. A double negative meant to be a positive, for example, isn't "illogical" (modern French and ancient Greek use them). According to Standard English, writing "I ain't no fool" is merely—unless it is a joke, or speech in fictional dialogue—a social mistake, at least for the present, indicating incompetence in picking up the right fork (a tip, by the way, no extra charge: start from the outside and work inward). If Orwell and his ilk start using "I ain't no fool," no amount of schoolmistress "logic" can stand in the way of its imitation. In matters of taste in writing the only standard is the practice of good writers and the reaction of good readers. You know writers are "good" by reading them with delight. No surprise. Many things, from the standard of proof in number theory to the standard of skill in baton twirling, are matters of taste. You find out who is good by comparing good with bad.

A reader will, without knowing she's doing it, grade writers by stylistic competence. A violation of the rules of clarity and grace sends a signal of incompetence. If you start sentences habitually with "However," the reader will probably find that you are an incompetent writer in other ways too, because you probably will be. The violations are correlated with each other. It's a good bet that a writer who doesn't know how to express parallel ideas in parallel form, and doesn't care, will also not know how to avoid excessive summarization and anticipation, and doesn't care. It's about as good a bet that she will not know how to think, and doesn't care.

6

Classical Rhetoric Guides Even the Economical Writer

A longish piece of prose is made from bunches of paragraphs, which are made from bunches of sentences, which are made from bunches of words. Before you start a piece, choose a subject that fits the assignment yet also stirs something in your soul. You can't work soulfully on a subject unless you love it, or hate it, or at any rate can gin up such emotions for the time being. You should therefore do your economic history on the fashion industry and your political science on advertising, if they are your loves or hates.

Rules about whole pieces or paragraphs are most useful at the stage of first composition. Rules about sentences and words are most useful at the stages of revision. And some rules apply everywhere. It's good to be brief in the whole piece and in the single word, during both the midnight fever of composition and the morning chill of revision. Brevity is the soul of clarity too. Yet the rules of writing can be stuffed if necessary, as here, into boxes by diminishing size from whole piece to word.

What's needed is "a rhetoric" of expository prose, in the report or the essay or the student paper. By "rhetoric" I do not mean a frill, nor a device for lying—the politician's "heated rhetoric" at a news conference or the professor's "bad rhetoric" when arguing a weak scientific case. I mean by rhetoric the whole art of argument, which is its classical and correct meaning. It's the art, as the rhetorician and professor of English Wayne Booth put it, "of discovering warrantable beliefs and improving those beliefs in shared discourse" (Booth 1974, 59).

The three important parts of classical rhetoric were invention, arrangement, and style.

Invention, the framing of arguments in economics or literature or the business memo worth listening to, is the craft of economic or literary or business theory and of economic or literary or business observation. Bad craft makes for bad thinking. Theory and observation in economics, for example, as in many other statistical fields, have been wrecked by an official methodology unaware of its rhetoric (McCloskey 1998). Literary people, by contrast, have less trouble with the truth that ideas are metaphors and stories. Businesspeople or civil servants stand somewhere in the middle.

Arrangement is a part of rhetoric not much examined. A good deal of academic and bureaucratic prose implies that the only proper arrangement of a paper is introduction, outline of the rest of the paper, theory, model, results, suggestions for future research (since nothing ever quite works), and (again) summary. It is supposed to make social sciences more scientific to have a section titled "Data" or "Results." The wretched handbooks of official style, especially the American Psychological Association's *Publication Manual*, enforce the arrangement. One rarely sees experiments with alternative arrangements, such as dialogues or reports on the actual sequence of the author's discovery. The official arrangement does not tell what needs to be known — which experiments failed, what mathematics proved fruitless, why exactly the questions were asked in the way they were (Medawar 1964).

7 Fluency Can Be Achieved by Grit

The third branch of classical rhetoric, style, is easier to teach, and is what the present book teaches. Style begins with mere fluency, getting something down on paper. And it ends with revising again and again, until you've removed all the snares and blemishes.

You will have done some research (it is known as "reading" and "calculating" and "thinking") and are sitting down to write. Sitting down to write can be a problem, because then your subconscious, which is dismayed by the task of filling up blank screens or sheets of paper, suggests that it would be ever so much more fun to do the dishes or check the email. Time to go see Mary or John. Time to watch the basketball game. Time to get some fresh air. Don't. Sneak up on the task and surprise it with the ancient recipe for success in intellectual pursuits. Locate chair. Apply rear end to it. Locate writing implement. Use it. You may wish to increase the element of surprise by writing standing at a tall desk, or one of those desks that can be pulled upward to stand at.

One of the distractions is taste. The trouble with developing good taste in writing, which is the point of studying books like this one, is that you begin to find your stuff distasteful. Taste creates doubt. Waves of doubt — the conviction that everything you've done so far is rubbish — will wash over you from time to time. I write a lot, and every time I write anything, from a little book review for the *Wall Street Journal* up to a seven-hundred-page book of my own, I face what Christian theology calls "the dark night of the soul." Every writer does. (If she doesn't, she's probably a fool.) What am I actually trying to say? Isn't it all pretty stupid? (Hey, maybe it is.) How can I arrange my pathetically obvious points in some way that conceals how pathetically obvious they are? And so forth. The only help is a cheerful hope that more work will raise even the rubbish up to your newly acquired standards. Once achieved, you can re-raise the standards and acquire a better doubt at a still higher level of taste.

Buck up. Irrational cheerfulness is hard to teach but is good to have for any work, of writing or of the soul.

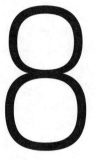

Write Early Rather Than Late

The teachable trick is getting a first draft. Don't wait until the research is done to begin writing, because writing, to repeat, is a way of thinking. Be writing all the time, working on a page or two here, a section there, a sentence, a crucial phrase. Research is writing, I say again, because you find the gaps and idiocies in your argument when you write it down. Or as my friend and frequent coauthor, the original "haiku economist" Stephen Ziliak, teaches in haiku-economic fashion (see the appendix):

> Write early, not late
> *Economical Writing*
> McZ number 8!

Manila folders were nice in the old days. In 1959 the American sociologist C. Wright Mills wrote an exhilarating essay, "On Intellectual Craftsmanship," in which he called the whole set of cards, folders, and so forth in which research was organized The File. The metaphor lives on in the digital age. "You must set up a file, which is, I suppose, a sociologist's way of saying: Keep a journal. Many creative writers keep journals. The sociologist's need for systematic reflection demands it" (Mills 1959, 196). So too does the economist's and the businessperson's and that of anyone working on a big project of writing. The file should become thick and rich, and should be occasionally dumped out and rearranged.

As a researcher you will have notes, bits of prose to be placed in the mosaic. It sometimes helps to give each note a title that states its gist, or at least a key word, though again the computer has made it easy to search entire files by a characteristic word. Though any writing surface from clay tablet to computer screen can hold the notes, when writing with a pen the best are white 4" × 6" cards lined on one side. With a word processor a good plan is just to spill out the notes as paragraphs, then print them out, cut them up with scissors, spread them on the table or floor, and seek the best arrangement. Use one idea per card or per paragraph, even if the idea is only a single line. It's a mistake to economize by cramming several ideas into a space. Paper is cheap. Memory on your computer is free.

Read through the file (which is invention) trying to see in it an outline (which is arrangement). The first outline will be broad and will doubtless not be the final one. Allocate the cards or strips of printed and cut-up paper to related stacks. Add notes reminding you of transitions and new ideas that occur as you ponder the file. Arrangement is like good statistical or historical or detective work, searching the data for patterns. It's like good dramatic work too, searching the audience for response. Your arrangement should be artful. Make it interesting.

Now set aside the broad outline, keeping it in mind. You need it as a goal to give the writing dramatic direction. You can change the outline, and should do so repeatedly as the piece takes shape and you think up cleverer ways of arranging. Pick a little part of the outline to write about today, perhaps an idea that came on you while reading. You need not start at the beginning, though it's sometimes difficult to resist the temptation. You can always throw away the pompous and vacuous introduction you write at first. The paper should end up as a story, because readers normally read from beginning to end.

Here's a word-processing trick for arrangement. It's a version of Mills's advice on paper items. Put a number at the beginning of each paragraph in the order you think might work, leaving a lot of numbers in between so there's room to insert items later. So: out of 999, put 100 on what you think is the first item in a good arrangement. But then you see that the next item you consider is actually better for the first position. All right, give it the number 050, say (notice that the numbers, somewhat irritatingly, have to have the same number of digits — in this case three — to be correctly sorted). The next item seems to work best late in the argument. All right, give it 900, leaving room for the 950 that you later see is even better. And so forth. Then select the whole set of notes and use the alphabetize function to sort them. This places your items in the order that seems to make sense. Now write them out, combining the paragraphs when necessary and making sure that the succession of them makes sense for your argument. Because you have them in a roughly sensible order, it's easy to move this or that paragraph around to get the order a little better. Eventually you can delete the numbers. It works.

Use the mad, creative "file" that is your brain. You need a certain intensity. Writing cannot be done entirely as a routine, like peeling potatoes. Before he met and fell in love with a Mr. Green, an English merchant resident at Köningsberg, the philosopher Immanuel Kant (1724– 1804), who was in his youth something of a man about town, declared that one could not write philosophy as though writing a bank check, routinely. (Then under the influence of Mr. Green, with whom he spent every afternoon and evening for twenty years, he learned to write philosophy as though writing a bank check, routinely, and revolutionized Western philosophy. Strange.)

If you get stuck, write a sub-outline, a narrower outline about the points you are going to write in the next few sentences or paragraphs, checking off the points mentally as you write. (Never stop for outlining or cleaning up or alphabetizing your library if you're *not* stuck.) Arrangement finds good outlines, from the level of the book down to the level of the paragraph. Later you should play around with the arrangement, moving whole paragraphs or sections around until they fit into a logic or a story. The points in all outlines from broad to narrow should be substantive, not formal: not "Introduction" or "Concluding Paragraph" but "Historians pay too little attention to the sexual division of labor" and "Housework should be included in national income," or in a telegraphic style, "div. lab." and "housewk & GDP." Keep a piece of paper at hand to try out turns of phrase or to note down ideas that occur in advance of their use.

When you get an inspiration, don't depend on your memory to keep it. A phrase or word will jog it. Don't let the nonroutine moment pass. There's plenty of time for routine. Pay the gas bill in a dull moment.

9 You Will Need Tools

You will need an outline on a sheet of paper sitting on your desk, or on your computer screen, covered with notes for revision, and some scratch paper for trying out things, and your file up on your screen. Don't worry about being neat, I repeat. Clean up in a dull moment.

You will need certain other bits of capital in abundance. Surely you have a word processor by now. An expensive and well-balanced fountain pen is old-fashioned but fun to use when the mood strikes. Likewise a classy little laptop that creates envy in everyone who sees you using it at Starbucks. Indulge yourself. You should find pleasure in exercising the tools of writing.

On the other hand, try not to become compulsive about equipment and procedures and surroundings. My father was also a professor and scholar. He could not work unless conditions were perfect, and so his child (that's me) venturing into the same occupation vowed to be more flexible. Hemingway used to sharpen forty pencils with a jackknife before beginning to write. He didn't write much, though a lot of it was pretty good. Dad didn't write much, either, though all of it was very good indeed. Be more flexible than Hemingway or my father if you can manage it. Look on yourself as an honest-to-goodness professional writer (which is what you are) who can do any job on command to deadline anywhere with any equipment whatever, Ernie Pyle pecking out newspaper dispatches on a portable typewriter from a foxhole on the Italian front in 1944. Most people compose these days at a computer screen. Some dictate into a tape recorder. Dragon lets you zap the dictation into writing on your own computer. I myself have just started using it for taking notes as I read books. It's brilliant, and you can buy "tape" recorders with Dragon installed. Some old fogies whom I dearly love still write out everything in longhand on big yellow legal pads. A new medium will change your style, perhaps for the better. Switching from medium to medium is worth trying, because each medium suggests new arrangements and new styles. If on your draft you change the typeface you will see it in a new light. As the professor of English and of composition Richard Lanham, a master of such things, advised, "toggle."

The next most important tool is a dictionary, or nowadays a site on the internet that is itself a good dictionary. Googling a word is a bad substitute for a good dictionary site. You have to choose the intelligent site over the dreck such as Wiktionary, Google, and Dictionary.com, all useless. One of the nondrecky ones, *Merriam-Webster*, defines *dreck*: "trash, rubbish." First English use 1922. Yiddish *drek* & German *Dreck*, from Middle High German *drec*; akin to Old English *threax*, rubbish. That's the sort of detail you need to understand a word. In the particular case, if you do not know that *dreck* is a recent borrowing from Yiddish (the Germanic language of Eastern European Jews, and therefore a source for American comedians), you will not be using it with the right nuance. Find a site that does a good job at word origins, which notes Americanisms (handy when writing to non-Americans), which gives easy-to-follow pronunciation guides (handy when speaking; some will read the word out loud), and which distinguishes levels of usage, that is, plain to fancy. The *Collins* site is pretty good, and free. In truth, no site does as well as, say, my favorite college-size paper dictionary, *Webster's New World Dictionary of the American Language.* The only truly serious source for the history of words is the great *Oxford English Dictionary* (1884–present), online but not free, except through university or other institutional sites.

A dictionary entry or a Google item, in other words, is for more than spelling. Pause, I urge you, to read the definitions and the word origins. Of course, part of the purpose is to not make embarrassing mistakes in usage. If you think *disinterested* means the same thing as *uninterested*, for instance, or that *infer* means "imply," or that one should say "the hoi polloi," you need to get acquainted with a dictionary and to start reading good writing with it at hand. Yet beyond what is meet and proper (look up *meet*, noting that in this sense it is related to *medical*), word lore will make you grow as a wordsmith. Learn to like words and to inquire about their backgrounds. It's a useful friendship and a joy.

English spelling would drive anybody nuts. The playwright George Bernard Shaw (1856–1950) noted once that you could spell the word *fish* in English as "ghoti" — *gh* as in *enough*, *o* as in *women*, and *ti* as in *nation*. Fish. It's amazing that anyone learns to spell according to Webster. In the sixteenth century nobody cared, and Shakespeare (Shakspere, Shakespere) spelt 'em az hee plees'd. But nowadays you must spell according to Webster or you look like a careless dolt. It is stupid and unfair, but that's the way things are. Students chronically misspell a few words, such as *receive* (remember Ms. Jones: *i* before *e* except after *c*; but what about *leisure*, *either*, *weird*, or for that matter, with the same -eird-, *Deirdre?*). *Separate* (pronounce the verb form carefully — "sepaRATE" — and you'll remember it). *Machine* and *schedule* (neither of which I could spell until graduate school, when I put them and twenty others up over my desk and forced myself to learn them).

The spellchecker is a great innovation. For Lord's sake use it. Never turn in anything to anyone, and certainly not to a boss or teacher whose opinion of you matters, or even (for practice) send casual emails, if you haven't spellchecked. It's usually automatic, which is a blessing. But remember that you have to choose *their* or *there* or *they're* for yourself, and scores of others such as *weather* or *whether* that slip through. There's no substitute for giving the paper that last, slow rereading. Mark it up with the few remaining corrections. No one will blame you if you leave a few proofing marks on the printed page. You're writing a report, not a copy of the Torah.

A thesaurus (Greek: "treasure") shows you the precise word within a more or less fuzzy region of the language. Unfortunately the so-called thesaurus available with most word processing programs is useless, because the choices are too few. But Theasaurus.com is exceptionally good. Put it up as an icon on your computer's desktop and use it to find the right word. You'll need the big old book form, *Roget's Thesaurus*, for other sorts of inquiries, such as measuring the disproportion in English between words for truth-telling and words for lying (lying wins, hands down).

"Proper words in proper places make the true definition of a style," said Jonathan Swift. Printed dictionaries of quotations (Bartlett's, Oxford, Penguin) have been made obsolete by the internet. Use the internet to find the precise words of a quotation within a more or less fuzzy memory: What exactly did Swift say? Wikipedia and the like are good for this, though watch out for quotations without sources. Websites of quotations tend to be compilations of what people *think* Ms. X said, not what she actually said.

It's instructive to keep a personal book of quotations, containing ideas you think are expressed well. This is called a "commonplace book," not because it's cheesy but because in classical rhetoric the commonly shared materials of invention, that is, of our culture, were called *loci communes*, literally "the common places" or "usual topics," *koinoi topoi* in Greek. Well kept, such a book as a computer file on your desktop can be the writer's journal of which Mills spoke.

10 Keep Your Spirits Up, Forge Ahead

Now start writing. Here I must become less helpful, not because I have been instructed to hold back the secrets of the trade but because creativity is scarce. Where exactly the next sentence comes from is not obvious. If it were obvious, then novels and reports to your boss could be written by machine.

If you can't think of anything to say, you'd better read more, converse more, calculate more, and in general research more. Most research, however, turns out to be irrelevant to the paper you finally write, which is another reason to mix writing with the researching early. The writing forces you to ask questions about what facts are strictly relevant. I used to show graduate students a six-foot stack of notes, which was *half* of the notes I took to write my first book, a snappy little production called *Economic Maturity and Entrepreneurial Decline: British Iron and Steel, 1879–1913* (get it and use it as a sleeping pill). The next sentence will sometimes reveal that you didn't do the right research. The guiding question in research (research, or invention, is not the main subject here, but no extra charge) is So What? Answer that question in every sentence, and you will become a great scholar, or a millionaire. Answer it once or twice in a ten-page paper or report, and you'll write a pretty good one.

If after all this, though, you still have nothing to say, then perhaps your mind is poorly stocked with ideas in general, those *koinoi topoi*. The solution is straightforward. Educate yourself. That is, live a life of wide experience, and spend big chunks of it reading the best our and other civilizations have to offer. Begin tonight. It's not too late to join the great conversation:

> As civilized human beings, we are the inheritors, neither of an inquiry about ourselves and the world, nor of an accumulating body of information, but of a conversation begun in the primeval forest and extended and made more articulate in the course of centuries. . . . Education, properly speaking, is an initiation . . . in which we acquire the intellectual and moral habits appropriate to conversation. (Oakeshott 1933, 198–99)

Anyway, say it. Saying it out loud will help. If people wrote more the way they spoke, their writing would have more vigor. If they spoke more the way they wrote, their speaking would have more precision. Francis Bacon wrote in 1625 in "Of Studies," "Reading maketh a full man [and woman, dear]; conference [that is, conversation] a ready man; and writing an exact man." Writing expresses personality, as does the speaking voice. The joke is that to write well you need merely to make yourself good and then write naturally. We are good when speaking to Mom or to a friend, and we commonly write well to them.

You hear a sentence when you read it out loud. It's a good rule not to write anything that would embarrass you to say out loud to the intended audience. In tutorials at Oxford and Cambridge the students had to read their writing out loud, and were thereby embarrassed if it was stupid. That's why British people of a certain class and generation did not write stupidities much, or if they did, wrote them with a certain charm. Don't write entirely silently, or you will write entirely stiffly. Good modern prose has the rhythms of actual speech — intelligent and honest actual speech, not the empty chatter of the sophomore trying to make it at the fraternity party or the waffling obscurity of the Labor Department bureaucrat trying to tell a lie about black teenage unemployment. We exaggerate the power of words to conceal a shameful intent. Generally the words expose it.

Regard the outline as an aid, not a master. When you get stuck, as you will, look at the outline, revise it, reread what you have written, reread the last bit you've written out loud, talk to yourself about where it is going, imagine explaining it to a friend, do actually explain it to a friend, try to imitate some way of speaking that Dennis or Maynard had, write a sentence parallel to the one just written, fill out the idea. Writing, like any form of thinking, flares and fizzles like a candle. Don't break off when on a burn. Be selfish about your little candle of creation.

Don't panic if the words don't come easily. Try changing your surroundings, though quickly. Then get back to work. Don't expect to write easily all the time. Few people do, and often enough if they do write easily is because they are not disciplining their writing with self-critical thinking. When I was in college I wrote well, because it seemed to me that the task was to come off as clever and not worry too much about whether the argument was true or not. I know scholars who stylistically never get over being in college, because they don't work at it. When I got to graduate school and determined that I was thenceforth to tell the whole truth and nothing but the truth, my writing style sharply deteriorated. I know plenty more scholars who stylistically never get over being in graduate school, because they don't work at it.

Keep the latest version of the manuscript in some form handy for rereading and revising. It's not a problem with word processing, entirely. (Though do save and save and save.) But you'll want to see the thing in hard copy occasionally too. Print it out and inspect it. When you are feeling dull, and especially when starting a session, reread a chunk of the draft, pen or typing fingers at the ready to insert, amend, revise, correct, cancel, delete, and improve. On a computer, scroll up a little and read what you've done as though you were a first-time reader, noting where your reading pace is checked by some difficulty of expression.

At the end of a session, or at any substantial break— that long snack I told you not to take — always write down your thoughts, however vague, about what will come next. This is a hot tip. Don't get up without doing it, even to answer nature's call. Write or type the notes directly onto the end of the text, where they can be looked at and crossed off as used. A few scraps will do, and will save half an hour of warming up when you start again. Jean Piaget, a titan of psychology (though not much of a stylist if one can judge from the English translations from his French), remarked once, "It's better to stop in the middle of the sentence. Then you don't waste time starting up" (Piaget and Bringuier 1980, 1). Paul Halmos urged the mathematical writer to plan the next session at the end of the present one (Halmos [1973] 1981, 28). After a session of writing, the ideas not yet used stand quasi-ready in the mind. Get them into that ideal storage medium, the file.

11 Speak to an Audience of Human Beings

Style, to say it once again, is rewriting, and rewriting can be learned in rules. Rewriting can be tiresome. Hemingway said, "Easy writing makes hard reading." He rewrote the last page of *Farewell to Arms* sixty times. Sixty. In sharpened pencil. The French novelist of the early nineteenth century Honoré Balzac rewrote his novels from printer's proofs as often as twenty-seven times, bankrupting himself with the expense (Lucas [1955] 2012, 270). Virginia Woolf rewrote parts of *The Waves* twenty times. Writing really well takes as much devotion as playing an instrument really well. The great violinist Giardini was asked how long it took him to learn how to play: "Twelve hours a day for twenty years" (Lucas [1955] 2012, 271). Yet in truth the practice hours are not as stressful as the performances. Once you are equipped with a technique for doing revision well, much of the rewriting will not hurt much. Rewriting for style does not have the anxiety of invention and arrangement — the anxiety that you will not be able to produce anything at all.

Look your audience directly in the eyes. Be honest with them. Ask who they are, aim the draft toward them, and keep hauling yourself back to facing them in revisions. Choose a reader and stick with her. There's no point in telling your reader in a paper on the oil industry that oil is a black, burnable fluid, then turning to a higher exposition that assumes the reader is a sentient adult, or for that matter an organic chemist. If you've started with a preschooler as an implied reader, you have to keep her around.

Some find it best to choose an implied reader of imagination. Others find it best to choose a real person, such as Richard Sutch or good old Professor Smith or the friend down the hall. It is healthy discipline to be haunted by people with high standards (but with some sympathy for the enterprise) looking over your shoulder in imagination. It keeps the prose steady at one level of difficulty to imagine one master spirit. "How would Sutch see this?" If it embarrasses you, when you are imagining how Sutch would read it, the stuff *is* embarrassing.

I don't say it's easy to keep an implied reader in mind. I tell people to do it, but I don't do it very well myself. If you can manage it, though, you have a sweet tool for keeping your argument at one level. A trick that works for me is to rush over to revising my own prose right after reading some admirable prose in, say, the *New Yorker*. For a half hour or so you can pick up the good practices of good writing by listening to it in your inner ear. I dote on the philosopher the late Richard Rorty, for example, and find myself imitating his tic of starting sentences with "We bourgeois liberals," inviting the reader to adopt his line. If I read Jane Austen, as I often do, in the aftermath I find myself using comical little ironies set into the last word in the sentence, most famously in "It is a truth universally acknowledged, that a single man in possession of a good fortune must be in want of a wife." It is good to read your own work with good prose ringing in your ears. After all, there's enough bad prose ringing too. Get the good ring.

It wears out after the half hour, though, and you return to your own wretched habits. Oh well. Keep at it.

 **Avoid Boilerplate**

Your writing must be interesting. The requirement sounds harshly difficult. Few of us are great wits, and most of us know we aren't. But you can avoid some dullness by rule. Choosing yourself as the audience tends to dullness, since most of us uncritically admire even dull products of our own brains. A reasonably correct recitation of the history of prices and interest rates over the past ten years may strike its author as a remarkable intellectual achievement, filled with drama and novelty. But Richard Sutch, who knows it, and good old Professor Smith, who lived it, and the colleague down the hall who couldn't care less about it probably don't agree. Spare them. Restatements of the well-known bore readers. Routine mathematical passages bore readers. Get to the point that some skeptical but serious and somewhat sympathetic reader cares about, and stick to it.

Therefore, avoid boilerplate. Boilerplate in prose is all that is prefabricated and predictable. It's too common. (The metaphor "boilerplate" compares prefabricated bits of writing to the prefabricated steel plate used to make big boilers for steam engines, twenty big plates per boiler.) Excessive introduction and summarizing and anticipation is boilerplate. Redoing for a large number of repetitive cases what can be done just as well with a single well-chosen one is boilerplate. Inserting a metric conversion after a British measure, "3 feet (0.914 meters)," shows that you think your reader is an ignoramus, especially if you keep doing it every time one system is mentioned ("100 kilometers [62.1 miles]"). It shows that you are an ignoramus, too, and think it clever to know conversions that any moderately educated human already knows, or can remember at the first pass. The academic pose inspires boilerplate. Little is getting accomplished with theoretical chatter copied out of a textbook. Apply it to the case at hand. Don't repeat it.

Impenetrable theoretical utterances have prestige in academic life, and even enchant people with no academic pretensions, as the popularity of books by Jean-Paul Sartre shows (except *Anti-Semite and Jew* [1945]; read it). But no scientific advance can be expected from such games of obscurity. A young academic or bureaucrat will sacrifice any amount of clarity and relevance to show that she can play the game. The result is filigreed boilerplate. I understand the impulse to pretension, proving your technical savvy. But it's obscure and uncandid. An economist, for example, will write about the completeness of arbitrage in this way: "Consider two cities, A and B, trading an asset, X. If the prices of X are the same in market A and in market B, then arbitrage may be said to be complete." The clear way does not draw attention to its "theoretical" character at all: "New York and London in 1870 both had markets for Union Pacific bonds. The question is, did the bonds sell for pretty much the same in both places?" In literary studies or legal studies, or for that matter physical and biological studies, the temptations of pointless jargon are great. Try not to yield. The great physicist Richard Feynman and the great naturalist E. O. Wilson and the great philosopher

John Searle wrote even their technical writing in as open and unpretentious way as possible. Imitate the best.

Never start a paper with that all-purpose filler for the bankrupt imagination, "This paper . . ." Describing the art of writing book reviews, Jacques Barzun and Henry Graff note that "the opening statement takes the reader from where he presumably stands in point of knowledge and brings him to the book under review" (Barzun and Graff [1970] 2003, 272). Good advice at the beginning of anything. In feature journalism it's called the "hook." A paper showing that monopoly greatly reduces income might best start: "Every economist knows by now that monopoly greatly reduces income [which is where he presumably stands in point of knowledge]. Every economist appears to be mistaken [thus bringing him to the matter under review]." It bores the reader to begin "This paper discusses the evidence against a large effect of monopoly on income." The reader's impulse, fully justified by the tiresome stuff to follow, is to give up.

Another piece of boilerplate, attached to the early parts of most student papers and plenty of governmental reports, is "background," a polite word for padding, the material you collected that you later discovered was beside the point. It seems a shame not to use it, you say to yourself. And after all it gives the thing weight. Resist. Remember my six-foot stack that was half the notes I took for a short book. If you have read a lot and if you have been thinking through the question you began with, asking and answering one question after another, you will have plenty to say. If you haven't read a lot and did not think through the questions you are asking, you will have nothing to say. Few will be fooled. Remember that professors and bosses are experts in detecting lack of effort and lack of success. It's part of their job description. You might as well spare a tree.

Still another piece of boilerplate, and one that kills the momentum of most papers on the second page, is the table-of-contents paragraph: "The outline of this paper is as follows." Official handbooks such as the *APA Manual* and too many editors and referees demand it. Don't, please, please, for God's sake, don't. Ninety-nine out of a hundred readers skip to the substance, if they can find it. The one out of the hundred who pauses on the paragraph is wasting her time. She can't understand the paragraph until, like the author, she has read the paper, at which point she doesn't need it. Usually the table-of-contents paragraph has been written with no particular audience in mind, least of all the audience of first-time readers of the paper. But even when done well it lacks a purpose. You will never see it in good writing, unless inserted by an editor who doesn't know good writing. Weak writers defend it as a "roadmap." But you're a writer trying to keep your reader, not the American Automobile Association.

Therefore avoid overtures, and do not give elaborate summaries of what you have said. Never repeat without apologizing for it ("as I said earlier"; or merely "again"). Unless you apologize for your occasional repetitions, the reader thinks you have not noticed that they repeat, and will suspect that you have not thought through the arrangement. She'll be right.

If you find yourself apologizing too much, realize that you re repeating too much. Stop it.

On the other hand, never, ever, for Lord's sake, anticipate: "As we shall see." Anticipation is useless and irritating. Even a few good writers fall for it. But can you imagine Adam Gopnik or Mary McCarthy or Truman Capote penning "as we shall see"? Remember that the paper or report that took you days or a week to write will be read in an hour. You must reread in the rapid way to get the experience the reader will have, and to make the experience tolerable.

The writer who wishes to be readable does not clot her prose with traffic directions. She thinks hard about the arrangement, using the outline scratched at as she writes. Add headings afterward if you wish, especially ones with declarative sentences advancing the argument, like the chapter titles here. Your prose, however, should read well and clearly without the headings, or else it is not well and clearly written.

Control Your Tone

The tone of the writing and much of its clarity depend on choosing and then maintaining an appropriate implied author. You can't simply "be yourself" when you write, though you will probably do a more persuasive job if the implied author in your writing resembles you. You will be talking like a real person and will automatically call on your human instincts of politeness in the presence of other real people. Tone reveals the character you take on to be while writing, the persona (Latin for "dramatic mask") of the Enthusiastic Student, the Earnest Scientist, the Reasonable and Modest Journeyman, the Genius, the Math Jock, the Professor, the Breezy Journalist. Look at a piece of writing and ask what implied author it has in mind. The piece that works will have an author the reader can tolerate. Writing performs a little drama in which the writer chooses the roles. You can't abstain from making the choice. Writing, like teaching or social life, performs a job of acting.

Many times in your writing career, however, you will be required to be less than candid. It would be bad for a dean to tell everything in her memorandum — bad for the college, bad for the students. It's like the comic movie with Jim Carrey *Liar, Liar*, in which a lawyer suddenly by magic finds that for twenty-four hours he cannot stretch the truth about anything. Not good. The Scottish American philosopher Alasdair McIntyre noted once that when he was asked as a child to admire the new hat of a maiden aunt, candor would not have been kind. "Auntie, I'm sorry, but in truth it looks like someone stuck a bowl of fruit on your head." Also not good. If you are the VP for sales, you are not under oath to reveal in your advertising that the competitor's product is better and cheaper. The ethical problem sits right in the middle of the road. "Rhetoric" gets a bad name from such problem cases — of having to tell less than the truth for another worthy goal, the good of an otherwise good college or the good of an otherwise good company. Welcome to life's dilemmas.

Everyone struggles with tone — student and professor, employee and boss. The student will sometimes use an implied author encountered only in government forms, using phrases like "due to" and "period of time" and "views were opposing." No one really talks that way to their mother. Adopting the implied author of The Newspaper Reporter is a natural alternative, since much of the reading a student does is from news sites. The stuff will be snappy. But it's hard to tolerate outside the newspaper. A daily journalist writes for the one paragraph jolt. She'd better.

Out of stage fright, professors in many academic fields overuse the pompous and unintelligible implied author The Scientist. Have pity on them, and help them overcome their fear. C. Wright Mills's discussion of the problem of writing sociology is applicable to other academic writing:

> Such lack of ready intelligibility, I believe, usually has little or nothing to do with the complexity of subject matter, and nothing at all with profundity of thought. It has to do almost entirely with certain confusions of the academic writer about his own status. . . . [Because

the academic writer in America] feels his own lack of public position, he often puts the claim for his own status before his claim for the attention of the reader to what he is saying. . . . To overcome the academic prose you have first to overcome the academic pose. . . . Clarify your answer to these important questions: (1) How difficult and complex after all is my subject? (2) When I write, what status am I claiming for myself? (3) For whom am I trying to write? (Mills 1959, 218–19)

In other words, what spoils academic writing is lack of confidence.

It's really not that difficult to explain in plain words to smart people willing to pay attention a Malthusian demographic model or the logic of preference in voting or why tariffs tax ourselves. A reader of a student research paper or a professional journal or a report to the boss is smart and willing. You must decide to be understood and worry some other time about being admired. Do not try to impress people who already understand the argument (they will not be impressed). Try to explain it in a reasonable tone to people who do not now understand. Your roommate is a good choice of audience, or your colleague. Neither will stand still for fakery. If you can't explain it to your boyfriend or your uncle, you probably don't understand it yourself.

Tone of writing is like tone of voice. It is personality expressed in prose. Writers would do better to reveal more of their character in their writing, or at any rate more of some attractive persona they are taking on while writing. A college teacher on the whole likes students, or else she would be selling insurance. So don't worry. Be nice, but not servile or pompous. Similar words of comfort apply to the professor herself. Relax. Take off the mask of The Scientist. You're lovable. Really.

The worst mistake is to be unpleasant. If you yell at people they will walk away, in reading as at a dorm party. Avoid invective, in formal prose and in blog posts. It undercuts your standing to speak. "This is pure nonsense," "there is absolutely no evidence for this view," "the hypothesis is fanciful" are fun phrases to write, satisfying to the writer as only political and intellectual passion can be. But they arouse the suspicion that the argument needed a passionate tone to overcome its weakness. An angry persona seldom works. As the great economist, sociologist, philosopher, and political scientist Adam Smith (1723–90) put it in his first of his two great books, *The Theory of Moral Sentiments*, "There are some passions of which the expressions excite no sort of sympathy, but . . . serve rather to disgust and provoke us against them. The furious behavior of an angry man is more likely to exasperate us against himself than against his enemies" (Smith [1759–90] 1976–82, 1.1.7). So watch it.

Tone is transmitted by adverbs, those "-ly" words that drive up the emotional pressure of verbs or adjectives. Run your pen through or select and delete each *very*. Most things aren't very. *Absolutely*, *purely*, and the like are the same. Most things aren't absolute or pure, and to claim they are gives a falsely emphatic tone. Watch out for pointless or excessive repeating. Once is enough. Thus in "endless attempts to extract higher wages by piling constraints on the wage bargain" the "endless" and "piling" have the same emotional force, the disapproval of an excess. Choose one, such as by dropping "endless."

Literally, by the way, is routinely misused, as when a federal judge said that the a presidential administration was "literally and figuratively declaring war on the Special

Prosecutor." The word means "actually, in truth, in actual fact." Yet no tanks or cannons were drawn up around the special prosecutor's office. The judge meant "Wow, I really feel this strongly!! I want to scream about it!" Screaming is not speaking well.

Keep your opinions, unless relevant to what you re arguing, pretty much to yourself. Strunk and White warn that "to air one's views gratuitously . . . is to imply that the demand for them is brisk" (Strunk and White 1979, 80). To air them intemperately reduces whatever demand there is. A comical example of what can go wrong with verbal abuse is "These very tendentious arguments are false." The writer meant "tenuous" (look it up). But even had she said "tenuous," the word *these* gives the reader the fleeting and hilarious impression that the writer was characterizing her *own* arguments, not the victim's. Tenuous and tendentious indeed.

Wit compensates for tendentiousness, as in the literary careers of the journalist H. L. Mencken and other satirists. Mencken's railings against the "boobocracy," as he called the government and public opinion, were made less tiresome by rhetorical coyness, ducking behind self-repudiating exaggeration or arch understatement. The reader allows such a writer more room to be opinionated because his opinions are so amusingly expressed. The great poet and classicist A. E. Housman (1859–1936) once devised a formula for attacking an inferior critic—before he knew who would be the actual victim (yes, he eventually did use it): "The one merit that Professor X's Latin criticism has is that there is so little of it." Opera singers will say, "She has a small voice, but it's ugly." Funny.

Most academic and business and bureaucratic prose could use more humor. There is nothing unscientific in self-deprecating jokes about the sample size, and noth-

ing unscholarly in dry wit about the failings of intellectual opponents. Even a pun can bring cheer to a teaching
assistant working through the fifty-fourth student paper,
or a chief in the federal government reading the tenth report on a new dam. A writer must entertain if she is to be
read. Only third-rate scholars, ineffective executives, and
C– students are so worried about the pose that they insist
on their dignity. The Nobel laureate and very good writer
Robert Solow (1924–), even though an economist, said of
economic prose:

> Personality is eliminated from journal articles because
> it's felt to be "unscientific." An author is proposing a
> hypothesis, testing a hypothesis, proving a theorem,
> not persuading the reader that this is a better way of
> thinking about X than that. Writing would be better
> if more of us saw economics as a way of organizing
> thoughts and perceptions about economic life rather
> than as a poor imitation of physics. (Solow 1981)

14 A Paragraph Should Have a Point

So much for the piece as a whole. Turn then to the paragraph. (I'm not much enjoying the principle of arrangement I've imposed here: piece-paragraph-sentence-word. Arrangement is not my strong point.) The paragraph should be a more or less complete discussion of one topic.

To sustain interest in any piece of writing, the reader needs to keep learning something. Don't let a paragraph go by in which you do not tell the reader something she doesn't know or doesn't at present believe. It needn't be a big fact or a gob-smacking idea every time. It can be a surprising detail. Or a fresh short quotation from another writer (you are a writer). But it has to be there, or she will start skipping what you've written. Notice that as a reader of modern news stories you skip over the tedious setting of the scene to get to the actual news. (The last sentence is an instance: you didn't realize, did you, that the old and good journalistic formula of the "lead" answering in the first paragraph what, when, who, why has been abandoned nowadays by schools of journalism in favor of "John was walking his dog one sunny day"?)

Paragraphing is punctuation, similar to stanzas in poetry or rock music. You will want occasionally to pause for various reasons, having completed a bit of discussion, shifting the tone perhaps or simply giving the reader a break. And here's a brilliant trick on the paragraph I learned from a colleague in the Department of English, Gerald Graff (past president of the Modern Language Association, etc., etc.): make the last sentence a simple, street-talk encapsulation or punctuation of what you've been saying, a sentence Mom could understand instantly. The paragraph can be as technical as you want as long as in the last sentence you come down a notch or two. Try it (I do, frequently, and will now do it here). It'll make your paragraph sing.

The stanza/paragraphs can't be too long. It exhausts the reader.

Paragraphs, though, should not be too short either. The same is true of sentences.

Short paragraphs give a breathless quality to the writing.

News writers, especially in sports stories, often write in one-sentence paragraphs.

For the sheer excitement of it.

It's a cheap trick.

Big quotations (in a block if more than four typed lines, always indented, with no quotation marks around the whole) have two legitimate jobs. They can give the devil his due. If you plan to rip to pieces a particular argument, then you should quote it in reasonable detail, to give at least the impression of being fair. Criticism that is only mild, however, can't follow a big quote. You must proceed to rip it to pieces, word by word. Otherwise the reader feels that the effort of settling into a new style for a bit has not been worthwhile.

And block quotations can give an angel her voice. If the excellent economist Armen Alchian or the excellent political scientist Judith Shklar said in over four printed lines something *strikingly* well expressed with which you entirely agree (for example, the quote from Solow I gave above), then you do not hurt your case by repeating what they said and gaining from their excellence. Routine explanations in other people's words, though, do not belong anywhere, whether in long or short quotations. They convey the impression that you think with your scissors, and not very well.

A word about plagiarism. Don't. Plagiarism is using other people's turns of phrase with the intent of claiming them as your own. Please, please don't. It's childish and immoral. The worst students sometimes do it out of desperation on the night before the paper is due (see above, chapter 8, "Write Early Rather Than Late"), then claim that they didn't understand the rules about plagiarism. You bet. It's a serious offense, and in a well-run college it results in expulsion. No college paper can be fashioned by stringing together passages from other writers. Your teachers and your bosses know you can read, at least in the sense of spelling out the words. They want you to learn how to think and write. Please help them. Anyway, nowadays with online search programs you are likely to get caught. Bigtime politicians have been caught doing it too, setting a horrible example for college students and government workers. The same is true of the wretched online paper-writing services, though there the politicians have a leg up. They have their own speechwriters, their own personal paper-writing service, so we never know whether they are intelligent or are merely good readers. For shame.

15 Make Tables, Graphs, Displayed Equations, and Labels on Images Readable by Themselves

The unintelligible tables and graphs in quantitative fields show how little academic and business writers care about expression. Tables and graphs are writing, and the usual rules of writing therefore apply. Bear your audience in mind. Try to be clear. Be brief. Ask: "Are these data necessary? Would I drone on in a similar way in prose?" No reader wants the annual figures of income between 1900 and 1980 when the issue is the growth of income over the whole span. The reader wants statistics given in the simplest form consistent with their use. The eight digits generated by the average calculator accomplish nothing. Who wants to read 3.14159256 when $3\frac{1}{7}$ denotes the number well enough without making the reader stop to grasp a stream of numbers? The point is widely misunderstood. (For economics and similar fields read Oskar Morgenstern, *On the Accuracy of Economic Observations*, 2nd ed. [1963], chapter 1.) For most questions we need only rough figures, such as those from Barbara Hanawalt (1979) and John Mueller (1989) and Steven Pinker (2011) indicating that murder and mayhem were much more common long ago than nowadays. 3.14159256 times more common.

Titles and headings in tables should be as close to self-explanatory as possible. The rule is that the reader should be able to understand the point being made by the table without referring to the main text. What? You don't know the point of the table and have not expressed it in a declarative sentence in its title? Well, then: think again. In competently edited magazines and newspapers you will see the rule being followed. In headings of tables you should use words, not computer acronyms. Remember: you're trying to be clear, not to be Phony Scientific. A column labeled "LPDOM" requires a step of translation to get to the meaning: "Logarithm of the Domestic Price." You want people to understand your stuff, not to jump through mental hoops.

The same principles should guide graphs and diagrams. Edward R. Tufte's *The Visual Display of Quantitative Information* (1983), one of the great nonfiction books of the past fifty years, demonstrates such precepts as "Mobilize every graphical element, perhaps several times over, to show the data" (Tufte 1983, 139; Tufte is not to be taken as a guide to writing well). Everyone who uses tables or graphs should buy and study Tufte's book, and then reward themselves by getting his second book, *Envisioning Information* (1990), and all the rest. Tufte warns you not to use "chart junk," that is, colors and shading and lined boxes that signify only a desire to ornament pointlessly. Have a point, he says.

And Deirdre's Rules: use titles for diagrams and for tables that announce their theme, such as "All Conferences Should Happen in the Midwest" instead of "A Model of Transport Costs." Use meaningful, spelled-out names for lines, points, and areas, not alphanumeric monstrosities: "Rich Budget Line" instead of "Locus QuERtY." You'll find it easier to follow your own argument and will be less likely to produce graphical nonsense. The same things can be said of displayed equations, if you are in a field that uses them. It's clearer and no less scientific to say "the regression was Quantity of Grain = 3.56 + 5.6 (Price of Grain) – 3.8 (Real Income)" than "the regression was Q = 3.56 + 5.6P – 3.8Y, where Q is quantity of grain, P its price, and Y real income."

Anyone can retrieve the algebra from the words, but the reverse is pointlessly harder. The retrieval is hard even for professional mathematicians. The set theorist Paul Halmos said: "The author had to code his thought in [symbols] (*I deny that anybody thinks in [such] terms*), and the reader has to decode" ([1973] 1981, 38, italics mine). Stanislav Ulam, with many other mathematicians, complains of the raising of the symbolic ante: "I am turned off when I see only formulas and symbols, and little text. It is too laborious for me to look at such pages not knowing what to concentrate on" (1976, 275). Tables, graphs, diagrams, and displayed equations should elucidate the argument, not obscure it.

Likewise in humanistic fields. Be clear. Ye olde spellin conventions copied laboriously from the source are not clear. Modernize the spelling and punctuation, following, for example, the editors of the Oxford Shakespeare, who cannot be accused of being inadequately scholarly. The past is a foreign country, but the foreignness should be exhibited in its strange behavior and strange ideas, not in its conventions of printing. The Olde Englishy convention, often enforced by the pedants, does not appear of course in quotations *translated* from the French or Spanish or whatever, imparting the strange impression that only native speakers of English wrote in Odde Capitales and Peculiare Spelings.

16 Footnotes and Other "Scholarly" Tics Are Pedantic

A footnote should be subordinate. That is why it is at the foot. In student and especially in academic writing, however, the most important work sometimes gets done in the small print at the bottom of the page. In economics the worst sustained example is Joseph Schumpeter's *History of Economic Analysis* (1954), in which the liveliest prose and the strongest points occur toward the end of footnotes spilling over three pages. Footnotes should not be used as a substitute for good arrangement. If the idea doesn't fit maybe it doesn't belong. Anything worth saying in your essay or report is worth saying in the main text. If it's not worth saying, drop it. Cluttering the main text with little side trips will break up the flow of ideas, like the footnote attached to this sentence.[1]

Footnotes should guide the reader to the sources. That is all. When they strain to do something else they get into trouble. And your attempt to assume the mantle of The

---

1. Inviting the reader to look away is not wise. Practically never is it a good idea to do what this note does, breaking a sentence. It should have been woven into the text, if it said anything, which it does not. Aren't you annoyed that I made you look down? Waste of time, yes? An amusing footnote on the matter, viewing it more cheerfully, is G. W. Bowersock, "The Art of the Footnote" (1983/1984).

Scholar looks foolish when the best you can do is cite the textbook. Some editors, as for example at student-edited law reviews, will insist that you footnote, or cite, quotations taken from the commonplaces of our culture, which in graceful prose are usually not in quotation marks. After a passage on whether a corporation is a legal person, the student editors want you to attach to a sentence such as "The question is to be or not to be" a citation (Shakespeare, *Hamlet*, act 3, scene 1). It doesn't pass the LOL test.

Citing whole books and articles without pointing to the exact page is a disease in modern nonfiction writing, spread by the author-date citation (used in the present book: for shame, for shame). By not bothering to find the page the quoter misses the chance to reread, and to re-think, and to find out if she in fact got it right. An author-date citation such as "(Fish 2001)" gives the reader no way to build on Stanley's wisdom, or his folly, or to check to see if you got it straight, or he did.

17 Make Your Writing Cohere

Behind rules on what to avoid lies a rule on what to seek. It's the Rule of Coherence. Make writing hang together. The reader can understand writing that hangs together, from the level of phrases up to entire books. She can't understand writing filled with irrelevancies.

Look again at the paragraph I just wrote. It's no masterpiece, but you probably grasped it without much effort. Each sentence is linked to the previous one. The first promises a rule to seek. The second names it, repeating the word *rule*. The next tells what the rule is, and uses the word *writing* for the first of three times, and the phrase *hang together* for the first of two. The sentence suggests why it is a good rule, reusing *hang together*, and introduces a character called "the reader," saying that she "can understand" certain writing. The final sentence emphasizes the point by putting it the other way, saying what writing she will *not* understand. The paragraph itself hangs together and is easily grasped.

Mathematicians would call it "transitive" writing. To do it you must violate the schoolmarm's rule of not repeating words. Verily, you must repeat them, linking the sentences and using pronouns like *it* and *them* to relieve monotony. The linkages can be tied neatly, if not too often, by repeating words with the same root in different forms, as was just done with the verb *linking* in the previous sentence and the noun *linkages* in this. In classical rhetoric the figure is called "polyptoton." Other tricks of cohesion also rely on repetition. In the present paragraph, for instance the word *repetition* is repeated right to the end in various forms: *repetition, repeating, repeat, repeating, repetition.*

If you draw on these tricks, you will be less likely to fill your paragraphs with irrelevancies. (AB)(BC)(CD) looks nice, is easy to understand, and is probably reasonable; (ABZYZ) (MNOP) (BJKL) looks ugly, is impossible to understand, and is probably nonsense. A newspaper editor once gave advice to a cub reporter: "It doesn't much matter what your first sentence is. It doesn't even much matter what the second is. But the third damn well better follow from the first and second." (AB)(CD)(BDE). If you once start a way of talking — a metaphor of birth in economic development or a tone of patient explanation to an idiot — you have to carry it through, making the third sentence follow from the others. Reread what you have written again and again, unifying the tenses of the verbs, unifying the vocabulary, unifying the form. That's how to get unified, transitive paragraphs.

Yet a clumsy way to get transitive paragraphs begins each sentence with a linking word. Indeed, not only did good Latin prose in the age of Cicero have this feature, but also ancient Greek had it, even it seems in common speech. In English, however, it is not successful. Therefore many Ciceronian and Greek adverbs and conjunctions are untranslatable. To be sure, the impulse to coherence is commendable. But on the other hand (as must be getting clear by now), you tire of being pushed around by the writer, told when you are to take a sentence illustratively ("indeed"), adversatively ("yet," "however," "but"), sequentially ("furthermore, therefore"), or concessively ("to be sure"). You are crushed by clanking machinery such as the hideous "not only . . . but also." The phrase is a literal translation (called by linguists a "calque") of Ciceronian Latin, *non solum . . . sed etiam.* It is admired as a thrilling ornament by bad writers of English, who learned it in the seventh grade and have employed it enthusiastically ever after. Don't. It marks you as incompetent. The best writers never use it. English achieves coherence by repetition, not by frantic signaling. Repeat, gracefully, and your paragraphs will cohere.

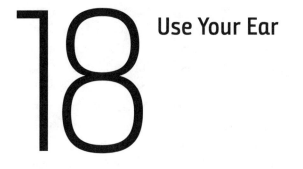

Use Your Ear

Prose has rhythms, some better than others. Abraham Lincoln and Martin Luther King Jr. knew rhythm in speech. The less gifted writer can at least avoid ugly rhythms by listening to what she has written. For instance, if every sentence is the same length and construction, the paragraph will become monotonous. If you have some dramatic reason for repeating the construction, the repetition is good. ("I have a dream.") If you have no good reason for doing so, the reader will feel misled. If you talk always in sentences of precut form, the paragraph will have a monotonous rhythm. If you have been paying attention recently, you will see what I mean.

The novelist John Gardner gave some good advice about variety in sentences (Gardner 1983, 104). Become self-conscious, he said, about how much you're putting into each part. An English sentence has grammatically speaking three parts: subject, verb, object. Thus: subject = "An English sentence"; verb = "has grammatically speaking" ("grammatically speaking" modifies the verb "has"); object = "three parts: subject, verb, object." Vary your sentences, Gardner suggested, by how much you put into each. And in each sentence choose only *one* of the three parts for elaboration. In the sentence just finished, the subject absent but understood = the imperative "you";

verb = "vary," modified by "how much you put into each"; object = "your sentences," simple, though not as simple as the subject. Gardner, who wrote pretty well, uncovered beautifully with his simple principle of the three sentence parts which I have just discussed and could discuss more if it were a good idea to do so, which it is not, because I've said enough already, the graceless rhythm that results from an overburdened sentence such as this one, in which every part has much too much in it, every phrase too much in the way of excessive adjectives and too many adverbs modifying its elements, which exhausts the reader and confuses her. Notice that you stopped paying attention about halfway through it. A sentence with too much in all three of its parts can ruin a paragraph. (That sentence follows Gardner's Rule: a complex subject ["A sentence with too much in all three of its parts"] connected to a simple verb ["can ruin"] and simple object ["a paragraph"].)

19 Write in Complete Sentences

Which leads to the sentence. That is not one. Such tricks should be attempted only occasionally, and only for a reason (here: a dramatic surprise, if corny). Write mainly in complete sentences. It isn't a matter of school grammar. It's a matter of not raising expectations that you don't fulfill. As a fluent speaker of English (or at least of your dialect), you know when a sentence is a sentence by asking whether it could stand as an isolated remark. The phrase "As a fluent speaker of English" could stand alone, but only as an answer to a question in a conversation. Socrates: "Tell me, Polus: how do you know what an English sentence is?" Polus: "As a fluent speaker of English." Ask if it could stand alone as an isolated remark. No, it can't. If someone came up to you on the street and said, "As a fluent speaker of English," you would expect her to continue. If, continuing to stare at you fixedly with a maniacal smile, she did not, you would edge carefully away.

20 Avoid Elegant Variation

The first duty in writing a sentence is to make it clear. Use one word to mean one thing. Get your words and things lined up and keep them that way. The positive rule is Strunk and White's: "Express parallel ideas in parallel form." [The next sentence illustrates:] The negative rule is Fowler's: "Avoid elegant variation." The two ideas are parallel and are expressed in parallel form: "The positive rule is" leads the reader to expect "The negative rule is." One hears every day the pair *positive* and *negative*. The reader gets what she expects. She can fit the novelties into what she already knows.

Elegant variation, on the contrary, uses many lovely words to mean one thing, with the result in the end that the reader, and even the writer, don't quite know what is being talked about. A paper on economic development used in two pages all these: "industrialization," "growing structural differentiation," "economic and social development," "social and economic development," "development," "economic growth," "growth," and "revolutionized means of production." With some effort you can see in context that they all meant about the same thing. The writer simply liked the sound of the differences and had studied elegance too young. Thus "the democratic **side** of the Allies concluded their antifascist war and began their anticommunist war against the other **half**" needs to repeat either "side" or "half": "the democratic half of the Allies concluded their antifascist war and began their anticommunist war against the other half." When uncertain what word or phrase to use, look back to the past few paragraphs for the same idea, and use the same word or phrase. Repeat! A writer on history wrote about the "indifferent harvests of 1815 and calamitous volume deficiencies of 1816." It takes a while to see that both mean about the same thing, a pretty simple thing. Notice that elegant variation often comes draped in five-dollar words ("growing structural differentiation" = new jobs in manufacturing; "indifferent harvests" = bad crops; "calamitous volume deficiencies" = very bad crops). Even my beloved *New Yorker*, once a byword for care in writing and editing, falls into it occasionally. In Mafia myth, "Osso *sailed* to Sicily and *founded* the Cosa Nostra, Mastrosso *travelled* to Naples and *set up* the Camorra, Carcognosso *went* to Calabria, where he *established* the 'Ngragheta." The writer didn't even bother to complete the parallelism of "and founded . . . and set up," which leads one to expect "and established." Come on, *New Yorker* editors: shape up.

People who write so seem to mistake the purpose of writing, believing it to be an opportunity for empty display. The seventh grade, they should realize, is over. Most people indulge in elegant variation out of correctable ignorance, as in "The new economic history is concerned not only with what happened but also with why events turned out as they did." Something is wrong, even aside from the pathetic ornament "not only . . . but also." The reader imagines fleetingly that "what happened" and the "events [that] turned out as they did" are different things. She must give thought as to whether they are. Elegant variation requires the pointless effort to see that "calamitous volume deficiencies" are the same thing as "very bad crops." It wastes the reader's attention in the solving of stupid puzzles. If the reader's attention strays a little — and it is always straying, a lot — she will come away from the sentence without knowing what it said.

But some repetition is pointless. Consider: "It is a place where work *gets done*. The new plan *gets done* by setting a new agenda." But the two "gets done" are not the same in meaning, so it's confusing to use the same phrase. You'll spot the pointless repetition by rereading cold what you've written. "Economics is not the only depressingly unscientific science in which ideology *runs* the show from behind the curtain." OK, but then two sentences later, "Ask the mother who *runs* into a burning house to save her child." Change the first "run" to, say, "controls." The two "runs" are different. Repetition is *not* good if it is pointless and careless. Thus "I am very much inclined to accept. I love Brazil, and very much want it to take the path of liberty." Besides violating the rule that "very" is very much overused in very first drafts in very many writers, the repeating of "very much" has no purpose of linking the sentences for clarity and grace.

But don't vary your words just to please Ms. Jones.

Watch How Each Word Connects with Others

Trimming away the elegant variation, like other rules of rewriting, does not make the writer's life easy. Most people's first drafts (including mine, for sure) are jammed with elegant variation, traffic signals, illogical sentences, nonsentences, misquotations, boilerplate, monotonies, and jingles. But easy writing, remember, makes hard reading. Samuel Johnson said a couple of centuries ago, "What is written without effort is in general read without pleasure."

Like effort in any work, such as sewing or auto repair, you must check and tighten, check and tighten. In short sessions the exercise will please you. The neat seam in a dress or the smooth joint in a fender revives the spirit worn from the effort. Still, before the end it wearies. Do nouns and verbs link successive sentences? Have I used one word to mean one thing? Is the verb in the sentence singular if the subject is? Have I used parallel forms to emphasize parallel ideas? Can I drop any word? Check and tighten. The care extends to tiny details. Test every sentence for redundancy. If you write, "The book often identifies what exactly was wrong with economic orthodoxy," you'll see on inspection that "often" and especially "identifies" and "exactly" all convey the idea of "regular precision." Drop all but one.

Again, you must choose repeatedly whether to carry

over words from one construction to its parallel. The technical term is *gapping*. You need to inspect every opportunity for gapping and choose whether to allow it. "It was new in the eighteenth century, and for two centuries has worked astonishingly well" to "It was new in the eighteenth century, and for two centuries it has worked astonishingly well." You have to judge every time which is easier to read. Or "to admire, or at least tolerate, business success" might be "to admire, or at least **to** tolerate, business success." Should you write "the beautiful and damned" or "the beautiful and the damned"? The only way to decide is to read it cold.

You have to choose how to modify nouns in parallels. "Smith and Milton Friedman, not Rousseau and Thomas Piketty" treats Adam Smith and Jean-Jacques Rousseau symmetrically, on the supposition that they are so famous that it would be insulting to the sophistication of the reader (if your reader in in fact sophisticated) to give their first names. But you do not leave off "Milton" and "Thomas," who are less known to history, unless the context is already about them and they have been introduced already. If you have one first name for the not-so-famous, you have to have the other too.

When you need to introduce someone you can add a phrase such as "the famous economist Milton Friedman." Such a phrase is called an "epithet," as in "swift-footed Achilles." But judge your reader to decide when she needs it. Inserting an epithet without "the" evokes the old habit of *Time* magazine: "famous economist Milton Friedman." It sounds, and was devised to sound, snappy, but is still not domesticated in the language. Don't.

Realize that in English gerunds or present participles ("supplying") and infinitives ("to supply") are substitutes for each other, though not perfectly so. You can say "Supplying a profitable forecast contradicts economics" or "To supply a profitable forecast contradicts economics." You can use the substitute to avoid a pointless repetition, when it is pointless, or to keep a parallelism.

Put modifiers — adjectives, adverbs, and whole -ing phrases, called properly in Ms. Jones's class "participles" — close to the word they modify. Otherwise they connect with other words and spoil the meaning. The passive, which is not to be recommended usually, does sometimes help keep a word and its descriptor close: "It began to dawn on me what the core of economics was actually saying — see *Human Action* and its Liberalism 1.0" — should be "It began to dawn on me what was actually being said in the core of economics — see *Human Action* and its Liberalism 1.0." The two have slightly different shades of meaning: is *Human Action* the core, or does it report on what the core is saying?

Other tools to line up word and thing are singulars and plurals, masculines and feminines. The Anglo-Saxon and Latin and Old French from which English descends had "inflections," that is endings, stuck onto verbs and nouns indicating all sorts of things, such as what they were doing in the sentence. In modern Spanish, for example, every noun indicates its gender, masculine or feminine. And every verb, too, is inflected, as in *hablar, hablo, hablamos.* Modern (and Middle) English has minimal inflection of verbs and does not have cases and gender for nouns (surviving only in pronouns: *he, she, it, her, him, his, hers, its, I, me*). English therefore doesn't often hitch related words together by the endings. Gender for pronouns and singular and plural for nouns and conjugations for verbs ("I go" and "I went") are all that remain.

Use the few resources of inflection that we have. The following sentence, for example, is ambiguous because "them" can refer to so many things: "Owners of the original and indestructible powers of the soil earned from them [powers or owners?] pure rents, and that tenant farmers were willing to pay them [the rents? the owners? the powers?] indicates that these powers of the soil were useful." You can work out what it means, but remember that the object is not to write so that the reader can understand but so that he cannot misunderstand. The singulars and plurals here are not essential to the meaning, and so they can be exploited to make it clear: "An owner of the original and indestructible powers of the soil earned from them [now effortlessly unambiguous because it agrees with the only plural referent available: the powers] pure rents, and that the tenant farmers were willing to pay him [unambiguous: the owner] indicates that these powers of the soil were useful." The use of *she* alongside *he* can in like fashion become an advantage for clarity of reference as much as a blow for gender equality. If you assign gender to the two people you are talking about (as I do sometimes here to distinguish the writer from the reader, alternating which is which) then your reader will see what you mean.

Capitals are useful word-changers too. You can make a word into a concrete and Proper Noun by capitalizing it, which makes it concrete. It's easy to point at a named Thing. That's why arguments in economics and mathematics go by names, even by names of people: "the Coase Theorem" is more vivid than "the proposition that property rights matter to allocation in the case of high transaction costs" (which, incidentally, is the correct statement of the theorem, widely misunderstood in economics). Capitalization can be used nicely for referring to a Point in a diagram. Be careful, though. Capitals have an Ironic Air to them, which is Fun only in Moderation (I tend to use them Much Too Much, and in revision have to decapitalize).

22 Watch Punctuation

Another detail is punctuation. You might think punctuation would be easy, since English has only seven marks (excepting parentheses [and brackets, which are used for parentheses within parentheses, as here, or for your insertions into someone else's sentence by way of comment or clarification]). Every educated person should watch the Danish comedian Victor Borge's routine on noises appropriate for speaking the marks of punctuation. Look it up.

You should understand the old typewriting convention about spaces in typing after marks of punctuation. After a comma (,), semicolon (;), or colon (:), put one space before you start something new. After a period (.), question mark (?), or exclamation point (!), put two spaces. Just do it. Don't argue. It makes word processing, short of fancy spacing programs for desktop publishing, look better and read easier. The editor of a book or a journal article will remove the two spaces for publication in a book or journal, because she *does* have a (very) fancy spacing program. But your manuscript is not a book or journal article.

You should also understand, and forgive, the strange convention about how quotation marks go together with punctuation. Contrary to what you might think would be more natural, in publications printed in the United States "the close quote goes *outside* the comma or the period, thus." Look where the period is at the end of that last. In the author-date system, used here and in most academic writing in these degenerate days, it goes like "how one treats a quotation" (McCloskey 2019). Notice where the end quotation mark, the parentheses containing the citation, and the period are placed. You'll look silly if you do what first-year students do: "a quotation here followed by the close quotation mark and a period and then the lonely citation". (McCloskey 2000). Not evil: we're not talking child murder here, just picking up the wrong fork at a formal dinner. To protect your reputation as a cultivated person, don't do it.

But just to make things interesting, in British publications the period or comma usually goes *outside* "the punctuation mark". As in that last. And in British publications the quote marks themselves are *single* ('inverted commas' the Brits call them), whereas the Yanks use double ("blah blah blah"). "And a 'quotation' within a quotation uses the other one." Or in Britain, 'And a "quotation" within a quotation uses the other one.' Latin countries indicate quotations with « and », or with dashes. Spanish writers, oddly, put an inverted question mark (¿) at the beginning of a question. Well, perhaps not so odd. After all, ¿why wait until the end to be assured that the sentence is in fact a question? ¡And likewise for exclamations!

The period, aside from quotation, poses no problems. To understand the most notable use of it in English literature, however, you have to know that in the English of England it is called a "full stop." In the last sentence of their spoof history of England, *1066 and All That* (1930), Sellar and Yeatman write that after the First World War "America became Top Nation and history came to a."

The dash — used like this, a parenthesis spoken in a

louder tone of voice — can be overused to solve a problem with a badly organized sentence. I do it a lot in drafts. But it is not otherwise difficult. It's a super comma. An "em dash," the longer one, is not the same as the shorter "en dash," slightly longer than a hyphen. If you're not sure how to form one with your word processor, look it up. Anyway, use the em dash, because good writers do — but not so much as the American poet Emily Dickinson did, who used it for every other form of punctuation.

A lot of people are confused about the colon (:) and the semicolon (;). In academic writing both are grossly overused. The safest rule is that the colon indicates an illustration to follow: just like this. The semicolon indicates a parallel remark; it is (as here) a parallel addition. The colon (:) means roughly "to be specific." The semicolon (;) means roughly "likewise" or "also."

The semicolon is also used to mark off items in series when the items themselves are long. "Faith, hope, and charity" properly uses commas. But if each item were elaborated ("Charity, the greatest of these, the light of the world;" and similarly with each) you'd better use the semicolon as a super comma. You can see that the semicolon is also a period lite; you can hurry the pace a bit by splicing two sentences with a semicolon, as here. So the semicolon falls between comma and period. Remember the difference between colon and semicolon by noting that the semicolon contains both a comma and a period within it, a printed compromise.

I said that academics especially overuse both the colon and the semicolon. I do, for example, and between the second and the present third edition of the book I took out dozens of colons and semicolons, making the previously joined sentences into two separate ones. Doing so adds to clarity, though it does forgo chances to show how clever I am in keeping colons and semicolons straight. Clever Deirdre.

The comma. Here's where everyone gets confused or argumentative. You should adopt rigorously the so-called Oxford Comma, so called I suppose because required in writings of Oxford students. It's also called the "serial comma," like a murderer. "Faith, hope, and charity" (note the comma before "and"). Not "Faith, hope and charity," which gives the impression that faith is one thing and hope-and-charity viewed as one item is the other. Or perhaps Faith is a person being addressed about the virtues of hope and charity. Legal cases have turned on the presence or absence of the Oxford Comma. No joke, to the losing side.

Avoid the dread Comma Splice, I've just used one, I connected two sentences, now three, I intend to keep doing it, it will drive you crazy, it's a grade-school error, your boss will think you're a dope. The rule is that if both clauses could stand alone as separate sentences, then you need either a bigtime mark (period, semicolon, colon) or a conjunction or conjunctive phrase. "The citizens lived in fear, the result was poor economic growth" contains a comma splice. Change it to "The citizens lived in fear. The result was poor economic growth." or "The citizens lived in fear, and the result [serving as a conjunctive phrase] was poor economic growth." Yet I have found comma splices in the writings among others of Matthew Arnold, admitted as one of the masters of English prose in the nineteenth century. Avoiding them is a social custom all the way down.

Weak writers nowadays use too many commas, and use them by rule rather than by ear, probably because Ms. Jones told them to. It's no rule of life, for instance, that

"An if-clause always requires a comma after it" or "When a clause cannot stand alone it must be hedged with commas." In fact, such rules lead to a comma in nearly every sentence, and a consequent slowing of pace, for no gain in clarity. When applied too enthusiastically the rule-driven comma ends up separating subject from verb.

Notice that I *did* use a comma after the "In fact" in the sentence before last. But I didn't after "When applied too enthusiastically" in the next sentence. In revision the trick is to delete most commas before *the*, as I just did after "In revision," and did a couple of sentences earlier after "When applied too enthusiastically." I didn't do it after "In fact" in the earlier sentence because the next word was not *the*. The *the* signals a new phrase well enough without the clunk of a comma.

And yet one must not be dogmatic about the comma. It is easy to fall into silly rules, mine as well as thine. The best rule is to punctuate by ear rather than by rule, and to insert a comma, as after "rule" here, where the pause in speaking seems to want it. and especially when even you as a reader of your own writing get lost without it. Reread and when *you* stumble, you know something is wrong, often fixed by dropping in a comma. When you want your prose to be read slowly and deliberately, and you have signaled such a ponderous tone in other ways as well, use commas heavily. For most writing use them lightly. A story about Gustave Flaubert (1821–80), the great French novelist, tells of his friends coming to him and saying, "Come on, Gustave. We are going to the country for the weekend." "No, sorry," he replied, "I have to work on a chapter." They noticed him striking a comma from a sentence. On Sunday evening they came back, and asked what he had accomplished over the weekend. "I put back the comma."

23

The Order Around Switch Until It Good Sounds

Inflected languages have more freedom of order than English. In Latin *Homo canem mordet* means the same thing as *Canem mordet homo*, with only a difference of emphasis. Both mean "A man bites a dog." But in an uninflected language like Chinese or English, "man bites dog" and "dog bites man" are news items of different orders. Still, much can be done with the order of an English sentence. With the order of an English sentence much can be done. You can do much with the order of an English sentence. It's mainly a matter of ear. Proper words in proper places. Tinker with the sentence until it sounds good.

A problem comes with modifiers, especially the location of adverbs, which float freely in English. Which freely float in English. Which in English freely float. A phrase such as "which is again merely another notation for X" should be "which again is merely another notation for X." Moving the "again" prevents it from piling up against the other modifier. Or: "the elasticities are both with respect to the price" should be "both elasticities are with respect to the price." Until they work, try out the words in various places. In various places try out the words until they work. Try out the words in various places until they work. There. If you can't get them to work, give up the sentence as a bad idea.

You should cultivate the habit of mentally rearranging the order of words and phrases of every sentence you write. Rules, as usual, govern the rewriting. One rule or trick is to use so-called auxiliary verbs (*should, can, might, had, is,* etc.) to lessen clotting in the sentence. "Looking through a lens-shape magnified what you saw." Tough to read. "Looking through a lens-shape **would** magnify what you saw" is easier. The auxiliaries add a little water — not always a good idea, but here, yes. Another rule/trick of arrangement is to avoid breaking, as in this clause, the flow with parenthetical remarks. I do it all the time in drafts and then have to untangle the sentence in revision. Two possibilities: put the remark close to the word it's mostly closely related to, or put the remark at the end if it's important.

The most important rule of rearrangement of sentences is that the end is the place of emphasis. I wrote the sentence first as "The end of the sentence is the emphatic location," which put the emphasis on the word *location*. The reader leaves the sentence with the last word ringing in her mental ears. I wanted, however, to emphasize the idea of emphasis, not the idea of location. So I rewrote it as ". . . is the place of emphasis." You should examine every sentence to see whether the main idea comes at the end — or (which is second in emphasis) the beginning. Dump less important things in the middle, or in the trash. A corollary of the rule is that putting less important things at the end will weaken the sentence. It would be grammatical to write "That putting trivial things at the end will weaken the sentence is a corollary of the rule." Yet it shifts the emphasis to something already finished, the rule. The clearer way emphasizes the novelty, the idea of the weakened sentence, by putting it at the end.

Listen for sentences that are monotonously long; listen for straggling sentences, as in that foolish young man of Japan,

> Whose limericks never would scan.
> When asked why it was
> He replied, "It's because
> I always try to get as much into the very last line of my
> limericks as I ever possibly can."

Adding one more idea at the last minute causes straggling, which eventuates even in a perfectly grammatical sentence like the present, making the sentence hard to read, which will cause the reader to stop reading after she has tried a couple of sentences like this one, which straggle, straggle, straggle.

A strange but effective rule is to line up a series of words or phrases by increasing length. That is, the lengthy bits should be at the end, although the rule will often conflict with the rule of putting the important matter at the end. At a minimum you should be aware of length and try it out in different portions of the sentence. The success of the seventh-grade ornaments, the doublet and the triplet (use them sparingly: write with a rifle, not a shotgun), depends critically on shifting the longest portions to the end: "Keynes and the Keynesians" works, "The Keynesians and Keynes" does not. "Faith, hope, and charity" works. "Charity, faith, and hope" does not.

24 Read, Out Loud

Reading out loud is a powerful technique of revision. By reading out loud you hear your writing internally as others hear it, and if your ear is good you'll detect the bad spots. For instance, it's practically impossible to decide when to use contractions like *you'll* or *it's* in semiformal prose without reading the sentence out loud. By reading out loud, furthermore, you'll pick up unintentional rhymes (at times your lines will chime), which can be distracting and mirth provoking. Remember the rule: don't write anything that you would be embarrassed to read out loud to the intended audience. As usual, Papa Hemingway had it right: "The writer needs a built-in, shockproof bullshit detector." You know more about good taste in the language, and how to spot bullshit, than you think. If in rereading your writing out loud you blush to hear an over-fancy sentence or a jargony word, change it.

No one, though, knows everything just because she's an English-speaking citizen. The ear is trained by exercise. Read the best old books (only when books are old do we know whether they are the best; the bestsellers of today are mostly rubbish — for example, *Shades of Gray* or, worse, *The Da Vinci Code*). Take pleasure in the language of good literature. Read poetry out loud, lots of it, the best. Memorize some of it. You know the lyrics of scores of rock songs. That's poetry, sometimes pretty good poetry. So you might as well learn some of the other stuff too. If you stop reading good writing when you leave school, you will stop improving your ear. The ear even of an economist or calculator should ring with our English literature. Close study of *Time* magazine and the *Wall Street Journal* doesn't normally suffice as an education in literacy — although it must be admitted that journalists like Meg Greenfield, George Will, Dave Barry, and P. J. O'Rourke use the newspaper language admirably well and are good models. They got that way, though, by reading the real stuff, Shakespeare and Ring Lardner.

Use Verbs, Active Ones

Finally, words. The snappiest rules of good writing are about words. For instance, write with nouns and, especially, verbs, not with adjectives and adverbs. In revision the adjectives and adverbs should be the first to go. Delete as many as you can. Around 1830 the humorist and Anglican priest Sydney Smith wrote, "In composing, as a general rule, run your pen through every other word you have written; you have no idea what vigour it will give to your style." He might have followed his own advice more fully, and would have done so if writing nowadays:

> In composing [of course it's composing: that's what we're talking about, you dolt!], ~~as a general rule~~ [what would be the point of any other?], run your pen through every other word you have written [of course writing: again, that's what we're talking about, dear; and in any case, what else would you run a pen through? your finger?]; you have no idea what vigour it will give ~~to your style~~ [for goodness sake, how often do you have to repeat that you are talking about style?].

The result is "Run your pen through every other word; you have no idea what vigour it will give." In both Smith's version and mine the word *it* is ambiguous. It's not instantly clear what *it* refers to. But that's another matter. (So is the slight English English divergence from American English in the spelling of -or/-our words, such as *vigo[u]r* or *hono[u]r*.)

Use active verbs: not "Active verbs should be used," which is cowardice, hiding the user in the passive voice. Rather: "You should use active verbs." The imperative is a good substitute for the passive, especially for taking a reader through complex arguments: "Then divide both sides by x" instead of "Both sides are then divided by x."

Verbs make English. If you pick out active, accurate, and lively verbs, you will write in an active, accurate, and lively style. You should find the action in a sentence and express it in a verb. Expressing it in a phrase functioning as a noun saps vigor. The disease is called "nominalization," and it afflicts most academic prose (mine, for instance). The teacher of style Joseph Williams, who discusses nominalization at length, gives an example that might have come from any statistical field: "There is a data reanalysis need." The only verb is the colorless *is*, and the real action is buried in the nouns *need* and *reanalysis* (Williams (1981) 2016, 12). You can fix such a sentence by using verbs: "We must reanalyze our data." Or consider that "On the left, there is widespread disdain for profit-driven healthcare" should be "The left disdains profit-driven healthcare." Find the action and express it in a verb, as vivid as truth will bear. Thus "Self-interested exchange is a knowledge-generating process" should be "Self-interested exchange generates knowledge." Circle every *is* in your writing, and if the page looks like a bad case of acne, try to replace each *is* with a real action verb.

"There is" and "It is" often cause nominalization. (I wrote that first as "are often problems," then thought better and found the action and the result.) Notice that a real verb requires a real subject. You can't hide. (I wrote at first "**There is** nowhere to hide.) The "data reanalysis need," by contrast, merely exists, blessedly free from personal responsibility. The freedom from responsibility makes nominalization popular among bureaucrats. That's us, often, so don't sneer. Find the verb. You have no idea what vigor it will bring.

26 Avoid Words That Bad Writers Love

Because it's easy at the level of the single word to detect and punish crime, the legislative attitude toward prose reaches its heaven in lists of Bad Words. Some perfectly good English words have died this way: for instance, *ain't*. Good writers have mental lists of words to avoid. At a minimum certain words will tag you as incompetent simply because good writers have decided so. For example—though it's unfair to the inexperienced, and nothing whatever in the nature of the linguistic universe justifies it—you might as well know that in some company if you use *hopefully* to mean "I hope" you will be set down as a fool. "Hopefully General Booth entered heaven" is taken to mean "with hope," not "I hope."

If bad prose would drop *via, the process of, intra, and/or, hypothesize, respectively,* and (a strange one, this) *this,* the gain in clarity and grace would be big. If it would drop *at least minimal, process of, thus, overall, basic,* and *factor,* the world would be saved. The best practice provides the standard. Virginia Woolf would not have written *and/or* or *he/she,* because she wanted prose, not a diagram. Some others that I'm sure Virginia would have disliked appear in my personal list of

BAD WORDS

Vague nouns

concept: a vague, Latinate (that is, pretentiously derived from Latin), front-parlor word; consider *idea, notion,* or *thought.*

data: over- and misused. "Data" are plural, although the word is clearly on its way to becoming singular in the language. *Data* means "givens" in Latin, and that is how you should use it, not as a do-all synonym for *facts, statistics, information, observations,* and so forth. The word embodies, incidentally, a danger-ous attitude toward observation — that it is "given" by someone else — but the point here is one of style. *Datum* is one data, though only pedants use it.

function: in the sense of "role" is Latinate.

situation: vague. *Position* or *condition* is better, depend-ing on the meaning.

individuals: for plain "people."

agents: the same.

structure: vague. There are no obvious alternatives to structure because the word usually doesn't mean anything at all. On this and other similar words in the social sciences, see Machlup (1963) 1967.

process: usually empty, and can be struck out (some-times with its *the*) without changing the meaning: "the transition process" becomes plain "the transition." In a very few cases you can properly use the word. The *Washington Post* columnist Kathleen Parker wrote of the "football," the nuclear codes in a bag never more than a few feet from the president: "There's no red 'launch' button in the bag. Once the president sorts through his options and decides on a course of action, he launches a *process* — have you ever loved that word more? — including discussions with key military and civilian advisers, who may talk him out of the attack" (*Washington Post*, February 15, 2017).

the existence of X: strike it out, and just name the X.

time frame: means "time." It originates in the engineer's notion that "time" means "passage of time" alone and not "a point in time" (another engineering expression). But the notion is false.

the turn of the nineteenth century: Admit it. Every time you read such a way of referring to 1800 (or 1900 or whatever the hell it is), you have to stop to figure it out. Is it 1800? Or maybe 1900, since 19 is mentioned? Don't puzzle the reader, so don't use it.

Pretentious and Feeble Verbs

critique: elegant variation for "criticize" or "read critically" or "comment on."

implement: used in Washingtonese, a rich and foolish dialect.

comprise: fancy talk for "include" or "consist of."

analyze: over- and misused as a synonym for *discuss* or *examine*. Look it up in your dictionary. It meant in Greek "cut to pieces." Keep the Greek in mind when you use it, and your sentence will be more vivid.

hypothesize: for "suppose" or "expect." The word tags you as a barbarian (similar words: finalize, and/or, time frame).

finalize: boardroom talk. See hypothesize, which is academic boardroom talk.

state: in the mere sense of "say." Why not say *say*? State means "assert with conviction." It is overused by writers who have not thought through what action they are representing. Try *assert, argue, reply, believe*, and so forth.

try and do something: say "try to do something."
  Strangely, "try and" is common among educated
  English people. In the United States it is a marker of
  incompetence.
the reason was due to: try again.

Pointless Adjectives

former . . . latter; the above; the preceding: and other
  words that request the reader to look back to sort out
  the former and latter things. Don't require the reader
  to look back, because she will, and will lose her place.
  Never ask the reader to solve a puzzle, because she
  won't be able to and will get annoyed.
aforementioned: what are you writing, a will?
intra/inter: do not use. Do not present verbal puzzles to
  your reader. Everyone has to stop to figure out what
  these prefixes mean. Use *within* and *between*. *International* and *intramural* are fine, of course, being well
  domesticated. But "the inter- and intra-firm communication was weak" is silly fancy talk.
interesting: a weak word, made weak by its common
  sarcastic use and by its overuse by people with nothing
  to say about their subject except that it is interesting.
  It arouses the reader's sadism. Oh, you say it's "interesting," eh?
kind of / sort of / type of: vague, vague, vague. Use
  sparingly.

Useless Adverbs

fortunately, interestingly, etc.: cheap ways of introducing
  irrelevant opinion.
respectively: as in "Consumption and investment were
  90% and 10% of income, respectively." Why would

anyone reverse the correct order of the numbers? (Answer: someone who does not express parallel ideas in parallel form.) Drawing attention to the possible lack of parallelism by mentioning explicitly that it did not take place is a bad idea. When the list is longer, distribute the numbers directly; "Consumption was 85% of income, investment 10%, and government spending 5%."

very: The very general rule is to think very hard before using *very* very much, and to very often strike it out. Most things aren't very.

for convenience: as in, "For convenience, we will adopt the following notation." All writing should be for convenience. What would be the point of writing for inconvenience?

Often you'll find that adverbs can be dropped (look for words ending in *-ly*). They often convey your opinion, which only your mother actually cares about or admires.

Clumsy Conjunctions

due to: used very often by bad writers who want to avoid *by* or *because*, for reasons mysterious, probably attributable to Ms. Jones.

in terms of: compare due to, thus, and hence. Use traffic signals sparingly.

plus to mean *and*: use *and* until the language has finished changing plus into *and*, which will take another century or so. I know you use it when you talk. Well, speech can be improved by writing too.

The choice of words determines how you think. Take economics. (Please?) The vocabulary of economics, like other specialized vocabularies, is enriched by coinages and borrowings: the Laffer curve, the affluent society, the agency problem. Contrary to a widespread impression among noneconomists, though, understanding the vocabulary of economics is not the same as understanding economics. Indeed, noneconomists come equipped with their own vocabulary for the economy, which dominates their thinking about it. Call it Ersatz Economics. In the Ersatz Economics of the person in the street, prices start by "skyrocketing" (have you ever seen a skyrocket? what price do you know that goes off like that?). When "sellers outnumber buyers," prices fall from "exorbitant" or "gouging" levels down through "fair" and "just." If this "vicious cycle" goes on too long, though, they fall to "unfair" and "cutthroat," the result of "dumping." Likewise, the person in the street believes she knows that unions and "international corporations" have more "bargaining power" than do their victims, and therefore can "exploit" them. A consumer can "afford" medical care, maybe only "barely afford" it, "needs" housing, and views food as a "basic necessity." Business people maintain their "profit margins," probably "obscene" or "unwarranted," by "passing along" the cost of a higher wage, which causes workers to demand still higher wages, in a "spiral." The protection of the American worker's "living wage" from "unfair competition" by "cheap foreign labor" should be high on the nation's list of "priorities," as should be the "rebuilding" of our "collapsing" industrial "base."

No such locutions should pass the lips of a professional economist. Likewise in other fields. To write thoughtfully in economics or sociology or business or government you must clear your mind of such cant, just as to understand astronomy you must stop talking about the sun "rising."

27 Be Concrete

A good general rule for words is Be Concrete. A singular, for example, is more concrete than a plural (compare "Singular words are more concrete than plurals"). The singular calls up an imagine of the singular thing, standing bravely forward. Plurals call up a more or less baggy collection. Prefer "Au Bon Pain baguette" to "bread," "bread" to "widgets," and "widgets" to "X." That is, flee the abstract. Bad writers don't believe that the reader will understand that "Au Bon Pain baguette" can stand for any commodity or that "ships" can stand for all equipment. Secret codes use the principle that translation is easier in one direction than in the other. A reader finds it harder to translate abstractions down into concrete examples than to translate examples up into abstract principles. Much writing in business and the social sciences reads like a code. "%& * marginal# #$$ processof& %$ #@ #$ % !structure."

Most professionals develop into code breakers. To an economist there does seem to be much wrong with a sentence such as this: "Had capital and labor in 1860 embodied the same technology used in 1780, the increase in capital would barely have offset the fixity of land." But here is a better way: "Had the machines and men of 1860 embodied the same knowledge of how to spin cotton or move cargo as in 1780, the larger numbers of spindles and ships would have barely offset the fixity of land." In a paper on Australia the phrase "sheep and wheat" would do just fine in place of "natural resource–oriented exports." In a paper on history "Spanish prices began to rise before the treasure came" would do just fine in place of "the commencement of the Spanish Price Revolution antedated the inflow of treasure."

28 Be Plain

The encoding often uses five-dollar words to support a pose of The Scientist or The Scholar. "Latinate abstraction" is an example from my own writing a while ago. I apologize. The pose is pathetic. Science and scholarship depend on the quality of argument, not on the level of diction. "The integrative consequences of growing structural differentiation" means in human-being talk "the need for others that someone feels when he buys rather than bakes his bread." English evolved a thousand years ago from its Germanic version (called Anglo-Saxon) into Middle English after a big infusion from French — the Normans who conquered England in 1066 spoke a version of Old French. Around 1400, when Middle English became the language of educated people, it began to get a massive infusion of Latin-origin and even (ancient) Greek-origin words too. The well-worn Anglo-Saxon words (*need, someone, feels, buys, bread, bake*) have a concreteness through homely use that more recent and more scholarly coinages from Latin and Greek do not have (*integrative, consequences, structural, differentiation*: all directly from Latin, without even a domesticating sojourn in French). "Geographical and cultural factors function to spatially confine growth to specific regions for long periods of time" means in Anglo-

Saxon and Norman French "It's a good bet that once a place gets poor it will stay poor."

Yet five-dollar words sometimes amuse. In the hands of a master they transmit irony, as in the analysis of sports by the great American economist and sociologist Thorstein Veblen (1857–1929). He wrote that sports (which he thought idiotic—he preferred reading) "have the advantage that they afford a politely blameless outlet for energies that might otherwise not readily be diverted from some useful end." Ha, ha. But you've got to be Veblen to get away with such stuff. In most hands it's just Latin-fed polysyllabic baloney: "Thus, it is suggested, a deeper understanding of the conditions affecting the speed and ultimate extent of an innovation's diffusion is to be obtained only by explicitly analyzing the specific choice of technique problem which its advent would have presented to objectively dissimilar members of the relevant (historical) population of potential adopters." Come off it, Professor D.

A lot of jargon hides a five-cent thought in a five-dollar word. The writers have forgotten that it's jargon. "Current period responses" means "what people do now." "Complex lagged effects" means "the many things they do later." "Interim variation" means "change." "monitored back" means "told." Soldiers generate such stuff endlessly, some of it witty, some of it attempting to hide what is actually going on: "wingnut" for Air Force personnel; "shit on a shingle" for chipped beef on toast; yet also "enhanced interrogation technique" for torture. It's the hiding and the fancy talk that's wrong. The "time inconsistency problem" is the problem of changing one's mind. The "principal/agent problem" is what hirelings do or fail to do.

The great jargon-generating function is what may be

called the teutonism, such as *der Grossjargongenerating-funktion*. Germans actually invents words like these, with native roots that no doubt make them evocative to German speakers (classical Sanskrit did it too, using as many as twenty elements). Again, it does not suit the genius of modern English. Sociology after Talcott Parsons and bureaucrats in all ages make up piled-up phrases with gusto. A common one in economics is "private wealth-seeking activity," a tight prose knot. Untie it. "The activity of seeking wealth privately." When laid out in this way, with the liberal use of *of*, the phrase looks pretty flabby. "Private" is understood anyway, "activity of" is pointless (note that nothing happens when you strike out "activity of"). By the principle of untying the knot, what is left is "the seeking of wealth." Good.

Unknotting will introduce *of* a lot: "factor price equalization" is muddy, though a strikingly successful bit of mud; "the equalization of the prices of factors" is clearer, if straggling. Most teutonisms do not make it as attempts to coin new jargon. "Elastic credit supply expectations rise" is too much to ask of any reader. She must sort out which word goes with which, whether the supply or the expectations are elastic, and what is rising. Hyphens help but impose more notation. The reader can digest "the long-run balance of payments adjustment" much easier if it's put as "the adjustment of the balance of payments in the long run." The result is inelegant, but no less elegant than the original, and it is clearer. Here are more knots that the reader must stop to untie: "anti-quantity theory evidence"; "contractually uniform transaction cost"; "initial relative capital goods price shock"; "any crude mass expulsion of labor by parliamentary enclosure thesis"; "community decision making process"; "Cobb-Douglas production function estimation approach"; "alternative property rights schemes." When you find yourself piling up nouns and adjectives, trim.

The possessive, unless attached to a proper noun (Samuelson's genius, Gary's pride), is not used much by good writers. It's overused by bad writers, who delight in phrases like "the standard political scientist's model." The possessive is a teutonism generator and has the teutonic ambiguity: what's standard, the model or the political scientist? Sure, your reader can figure it out. But you're not supposed to leave a trail of puzzles.

Remember Sydney Smith running his pen through every other word. You should reexamine any phrase with more than one adjective, considering whether it might be better in leaner form. Watch especially for nouns used as adjectives. It is the genius of English to let verbs become nouns and nouns adjectives. Don't worry about that. You go to the club, get a go in cribbage, and hear that all systems are go at the Cape. What is objectionable is piling up these nounverbadjectives teutonically.

29 Avoid Cheap Typographical Tricks

Certain typographical devices need careful handling. Use these "devices" sparingly, they add an "air" of (henceforth "AO") Breathlessness or Solemnity or Coyness! The point is that they add something, instead of "letting it speak for itself" (LISFI). They are, so to speak, sound effects!!! The reader "understands" this, and doubts everything that is said!! LISFI is better. Using these "devices" instead of LISFI suggests that something is wrong with the prose as is. If to make your point clear you use *italics* (it would be <u>underlining</u> in writing by hand), it is probably because the sentence is not set up to give emphasis naturally. Fix it. If you use "quotation marks" all the time when not actually "quoting" someone, it is probable that you wish to "apologize" for the "wrong" word or to sneer at "it." Don't. It's impolite to cringe or to sneer.

Another objectionable practice is the acronym, such as "Modigliani and Miller (henceforth M&M)" or "purchasing power parity (PPP)." Besides introducing zany associations with candy and second-grade humor, acronyms pimple the page and add a burden of excess notation on the reader. The demands of the computer have worsened the situation. Resist, and remember that even expert mathematicians often find it hard to think in symbols. At teatime at the Princeton Institute for Advanced Study, Einstein's institute, a mathematician talks to another other by a little diagram with a finger on his hand, while chewing on a cookie. No symbols. An occasional GDP or CAB won't hurt anyone, but even such a commonplace among national income accounts as GDCF pains all but the most hardened. "Gross domestic capital formation" is fine once or twice to fix ideas, but then "capital formation" or (after all) plain "it" will do the job. Believe me: people will not keep slipping into thinking of it as NDCF or GCF or GC. The point is to be clear, not to "save space" (as the absurd justification for acronyms has it, absurd because the acronyms in most long reports will save a half dozen lines of print at most, less space for example than the pointless paragraph of the "roadmap"). As usual, good writers set the standard of what to do. You won't find Milton Friedman or Kenneth Arrow baffling their readers with LQWAGE and BBLUUBB. The bad writers often enough participate in fraud. In a Scott Adams cartoon strip (March 6, 2018) a manager advises Dilbert the engineer: "Your project summary needs more jargon and acronyms." In the next panel he explains why: "The goal is to make ourselves look smart while making the readers feel dumb." In the last, Dilbert asks, "But what about clarity?" to which the manager replies (because Dilbert's company always makes rubbishy electronics), "Clarity is not our friend on this one."

Another typographical trick is full-justifying the text, that is, lining up the right margin like the left, as though in book printing. In a piece meant for an academic audience, always use a ragged right margin (left justification). Just believe me on this one. The rule is a good example of the arbitrary, picking-up-the-correct-fork character of some rules. Justification makes it look to an academic audience like you value cute tricks with your computer more than the writing itself. And it often produces lines like this one. On the other hand, in business and governmental writing you should full-justify, because it is the practice in such honorable trades.

Pick up the fork that your tribe requires, short of actual barbarities.

30 Avoid This, That, These, Those

Another plague is this-ism. These bad writers think this reader needs those repeated reminders that it is this idea, not that other one, which is being discussed. Circle every *this* and *these* and *those* in your draft. You will be shocked by their number. The *this* points the reader back to the thing referred to, for no good reason. No writer wants her reader to look back, because looking back is looking away, interrupting the forward flow and leaving the reader looking for her place.

This-ism shows linguistic drift, happening without anyone noticing, as changes in language often do. Even those good writers are falling into this. Recall Wayne Booth's definition of rhetoric as the art "of discovering warrantable beliefs and improving those beliefs in shared discourse" (Booth 1974, 59). "Those beliefs." Hmm. Shame on you, Wayne. Plain "the beliefs" would do fine. In fact, better. The one blot in the excellent style book *They Say, I Say: The Moves That Matter in Academic Writing* by my colleagues in English at UIC Gerald Graff and Cathy Birkenstein is that at one point they recommend using *this* and *these* all over the place. Oy. Even I do it in first drafts — an indication that the Spirit of English is driving us in the matter. I've had to expunge numerous *this/these/*

those from this . . . uh . . . the new edition you are holding. Oh, well, maybe "this edition" is acceptable. But watch it.

In English it grows and grows. *This* and *that* and *those* are demonstrative pronouns, pointing words, on the way to becoming a definite article, *the*. Most languages (Slavic languages, ancient Latin, Chinese) don't have the definite article. *Le* and *la* in French, like *el* and *la* in Spanish, come from Latin *ille* and *illa* and meant "that one," pointing over there. The ancient Greeks went through a similar development from Homeric to Attic Greek of making pointing words into the definite article. But English and French and German and Swedish speakers already have a definite article. In English it's *the*. It is ultimately derived from a word in Indo-European (the language spoken about six thousand years ago from which many Indian and most European languages descended) meaning, of course, "that."

Often the plain *the* will do fine and keep the reader reading. The formula in revision is to ask of every *this*, *these, those* whether it might better be replaced by ether plain old *the* (the most common option) or *it*, or *such* (*a*). Try it out. It works, and stops you from driving the reader batty by insisting she look back for every noun. And consider anyway repeating the word represented by *this*. Graceful repetition, remember, brings clarity and unity to English prose.

Exercise: Read the following (or maybe "this") passage about an exhibition of ancient Chinese bronzes from the *Member Magazine* of the Art Institute of Chicago, for January/February 2018 (p. 11), even though written by highly literate historians of art, associated with a great museum:

> Exquisitely ornamented, **these** vessels were made
> to carry sacrificial offerings . . . . When they were

found by emperors centuries later, **these** spiritually
significant objects were seen as manifestations of a
heavenly mandate on a ruler. . . . **This** exhibition —
the first to explore how **these** exquisite objects
were collected . . . — presents a rare opportunity to
experience a large number of **these** works.

Well, maybe not *highly* literate — note the elegant variation of "vessels," objects," "works," and the exhibition-
speak exaggerations. A charitable reading would concede
that exaggerations come with the job. But not "**these** exaggerations" or "**this** job."

Above All, Look at Your Words

Beyond such matters of taste lie the idioms of English. You must write English, no easy task. The prepositions of English, for example, cause trouble. They are its substitute for the grammatical cases that inflected languages have attached to the endings or beginnings of works. Prepositions (*of, about, at, on, in, after,* etc.) often go better with one word than another. I know of no simple guides. You'll know by instinct, if you read a lot of good writing. Don't worry about it too much in the first or second revision. You'll notice in the third and fourth revisions that "the discussion *about* me doing" is better than "the discussion *of* me doing."

Try experimenting to get the prepositions right. Is it *by* an increase *of* supply or *because of* an increase *in* supply? God, and the best writers, know. Verbs often come preposition-enriched: write down, write up, write out, and the like. That is, prepositions can become adverbs. Pare the prepositions away if they are not essential. If you sense that you are using too many verbs-plus-prepositions you can sometimes lighten the ambiguity by choosing instead a verb that contains the idea itself. You "write down" a proverb, or you can "inscribe" it. They mean pretty much the same thing, though the single word usually comes from Latin (*in-scribo*, "I write down") in a higher register (which is high-register talk for fancy talk).

By the way, you will have noticed that word lore depends on learning a little about the history of the language. You don't have to become a historical linguist, but it's well worth your time as an educated person to learn some Latin and Greek. Much of English (and most of the daughters of Latin such as Spanish and French) comes from Latin, and many coinages of the past few centuries come from ancient Greek. Medical jargon uses Greek most insistently, and most insanely. You need to know that *-itis* on the end of a medical word means in Greek "inflammation of," or in other words, "we doctors have no idea what caused it, or how to treat it, but it sure looks red." I recommend Donald Ayers's *English Words from Latin and Greek Elements*. There are any number of texts on Latin and Greek. If you get to page 50 in any of them, you'll be wiser in using English.

Words often come in pairs. You "overcome," not "cure," your ignorance. One cures diseases but overcomes handicaps. Ignorance is an overcomable handicap. But thinking in word pairs sometimes leads to cliché. Flee the cliché when a more original word is precise and vivid. Observe what varied thoughts about "the pursuit of profit" are suggested by fleeing the cliché and looking into "seeking" or "finding" or "receiving" or "uncovering" or "bumping into" profit. The political philosopher and economist of the "Austrian" school of economics F. A. Hayek said that he came to understand the role of information in a market economy by thinking hard about a phrase his colleagues at the London School of Economics in the 1930s found merely funny. They laughed at the ignorant redundancy of the phrase "given data." As I've noted, the word *data* already means "givens" in Latin, and economists in the 1930s all knew a little Latin, if they had been minimally educated at school. "That led me, in part, to ask to whom were the data really given. To us [staff at the school], it was of course to nobody. . . . That's what led me, in the thirties, to the idea that the whole problem was the utilization of information dispersed among thousands of people and not possessed by anyone" (Hayek 1994, 147). New words suggest new thoughts. Word-thought is a tool of thinking.

One should think what a word literally means and what it connotes. English like all languages breeds metaphors, which then die in the sense that speakers forget that the expression is a metaphor and start believing that it is "literal." Sometimes the dead metaphors will sit up in their coffins to incongruous effect. A skilled writer examines words for their original meaning, to make sure that the metaphors remain dead or are at least brought to life in a decorous way. Are the words literally possible? "The indicators influenced the controls." How does an indicator influence a control? Someone wrote "the severity of the models." Punishments, not models, can be "severe." What he meant is that the models make assumptions that are hard to believe. He should have said it with a word like *unbelievability*.

Word lore never ends. The study of dictionaries and style books and the best writing of the ages will make you at least embarrassed to be ignorant, which is the beginning of wisdom. You should know that *however* works best in a secondary position, and therefore you should never start a sentence with it. Never, despite the looniness of Ms. Jones's rule that you should never start a sentence with *But* or *And*. You should know that "in this period" is usually redundant, that numbered lists are clumsy (I have used one to arrange my little book — for shame!), that "not only . . . but also" is a callow Latinism, that "due to" is bureaucratese, that use of "regarding X" or "in regard to X" is definite evidence of a bad education in the language.

Be of good cheer. You have plenty of company in such infelicities. We all have a lot to learn. I do. You do.

32 Use Standard Forms in Letters

Emails. Use standard rules of capitalization. Never "i went to boston." Yes, it's irritating to have to press Shift all the time. But not doing so makes you look like a self-indulgent little idiot. And if you don't know the standard rules of capitalization, for Lord's sake learn them. You are an adult, and it is no longer charming to write like you are still in the third grade.

On that point, by the way, many people nowadays have handwriting that makes it look like they are in the third grade. Cursive writing is dying and is no longer taught in many schools. So you print when you write. Fine. But develop an adult-looking set of print letters. It's not very hard to do, so do it. Otherwise your marginal comments on the boss's memo will look like you have just escaped from grade school. The advice applies especially to boys and men. Girls and women seem to take more care.

To get better at printing, write out your personal alphabet in lower- and uppercase letters, choosing nice-looking versions of each. For example, the lowercase "a" shaped just like this printed version is nicer looking than the *o* with a tail that stands for little *A* in cursive. Make your choice as you will, and then stick to it. (The only printed lowercase letter than would look strange in handwritten is *g*.) Especially, don't use little capitals as lowercase, such as a scrunched-up *r* for *r*. It takes about a week to learn to use lowercase letters and uppercase for their correct roles instead of mixing them. And learn in the (mere) week to rigorously extend the vertical tails of lowercase letters above the halfway line (*b, d, f, h, k, l, t*) and below the baseline (*g, j, p, q, y*). Never extend uppercase letters: *ALL OF THEM FILL THE LINE.*

Back to emails. Always reread an email slowly to check for typos. If you don't, the reader will have to deal with your tendency to type *R* when you mean *E*. And reread to cool the tone. You will never regret not sending an email the very moment you finish it. Wait a day, and reconsider whether you actually want to make an enemy for life.

Now as to form. *Never* start emails with "Hi Deirdre" or "Hi professor." You will do better with old people if you follow the conventions you were taught in school of old-style letters. If you were not taught in school, or missed that lesson, learn them. (In Norwegian, oddly, "Hi Deirdre" is entirely normal.) Open with "Dear Ms. McCloskey" or "Dear Professor McCloskey" (or still better, "Her Royal Majesty Deirdre McCloskey") followed by a colon : in a business letter, or a comma if somewhat less formal, and always a comma, "Dear Deirdre," if you are on a first-name basis. Then close on a new line with "Sincerely," if a formal letter, followed always by a comma, or if informal with "Regards," or if on intimate terms and you are a woman, "Love," or "Warm regards" if you are a man not actually in love with the person you are writing to, then on still another new line put your name — according to your familiarity, just your first name or your whole name.

If writing to a famous person you have not met, do not start with "You don't know me, but . . ." And if writing to a famous person you *have* met, do not say "You will not remember me, but . . ." You think it is properly humble.

Actually, it is emotionally coercive and childish and undignified, so I reckon you should not do it. Use the salutation to signal alleged familiarity ("Dear George") that the victim may have forgotten, or gently remind him: "It was so pleasant to meet you when . . ." If you have not met, introduce yourself, briefly: "I am a teacher of writing and simply *love* your *Economical Writing*." That'll do the trick.

Treat Speaking in Public as a Performance

In a middle-class occupation, I've noted, you are asked to write. But you are also asked to give speeches, or at least make interventions in a meeting. Speaking has rules too.

Learn to do it by doing it. I know personally the terror, because I have always stuttered (like Churchill, Marilyn Monroe, Senator Moynihan, and John Stossel; much less now, thank you very much). Early in college I did not want to be called on in class. I got over it then, and I haven't stopped yammering since. Now I am nerveless about talking to a thousand people, or on TV, though I still occasionally block on a word. Get used to it, I think to myself.

You can become similarly relaxed about public speaking, and should.

Having a small voice, hard to hear in the back row, is not, as you may think, an attractively modest habit. It is simply hard to hear, and irritating. Women especially must develop a strong voice if they are to get listened to by men (yes, I know: it's basically hopeless, and believe me, since 1995 I've experienced it!). The first woman British prime minister, Margaret Thatcher (1925–2013), sought speech therapy to get a *lower* voice. It was worth it. She was prime minster for eleven years.

Any speaking, like any writing, is a performance. You need to treat it theatrically. A young Dutch friend of mine, the daughter of friends in Holland, was very shy as a girl. When she came to live with me for a half year in Chicago, she decided to get over it and signed up for lessons in one of Chicago's famous improvisation schools. Imagine the strength of character it took. It worked brilliantly. You can do it with Toastmasters, a club teaching people how to do public speaking.

Never tell your audience the outline of what you are going to say. If you find yourself using sentences such as "I'm going to tell you about buzz, buzz, buzz," you are boring the audience and not helping it grasp what you're saying. Just *do* the buzz, buzz, buzz.

Never tell jokes unless you know for sure that you are gifted at such performances. Here's the test: do people regularly laugh uproariously at your jokes? If not, you are not a natural comic. Stop trying to be one.

Likewise, do not snicker or giggle nervously. Young men need to watch for snickering, young women for giggling. A teacher of English in Japan was being driven nuts by the inability of her young female students to try out an English phrase without engaging in self-deprecating tittering, because tittering ("tee hee hee!") is socially compulsory among young women in Japan. It was wrecking the lessons, and the young women were not learning anything. So she said, "No tittering. Instead, when we want to laugh we are going to do big, American-style laughing, at full volume. Ha, ha, ha!" The students got into the swing of things, and saw what their tittering was doing, and stopped it. And learned English.

Memorize what you are going to say. Not word for word, unless you have paralyzing stage fright (prediction: you will probably get over it), but as a matter of mastering what you are asserting, in outline. Then let your knowledge or passion about the subject fill in the gaps. Stand

and deliver. Try not to use written outlines, and *never, ever stand reading your PowerPoint with your back to the audience.* Notice how skilled politicians and other performers act. Imagine a stand-up comedian who kept looking at her written notes. Not clever.

A first-paragraph introduction of yourself, particularly if it is charming or very much to the point, is all right. I told you I stutter, so when I think the audience might become uncomfortable about it, I start by saying, "I have a speech defect [I stutter on the word *stutter*, so I can't say it more straightforwardly!], and you can either get used to it or run screaming from the room. It's a free country, so feel free. I won't break down crying." I'm trying to put the audience at ease. Because I also have a low voice for a woman, the little joke, not very funny but serving the purpose, covers two for one.

After such brief introductions, if they are absolutely necessary, *never again* talk about yourself. Talk about the subject. That's what the audience wants to know about. Not little you. The only exception would be if you have a personal experience to relate that is right on point. Or in the rare case when the subject *is* you, such as Socrates at his trial.

PowerPoint is evil, which is the title of a little squib by Edward Tufte that settles the issue. Look it up on the web. Death by PowerPoint has become the usual method of execution of audiences in the world.

34 Advice for Nonnative English Speakers

As an idiot mnonolingual myself, I am astonished at the courage it takes a nonnative speaker of English to write in it. In all humility, I want to help you. Mistakes in pronunciation that educated, nonnative, yet excellent speakers of English make include these:

RhhheTORicS. No. It's "**RET**-or-rik." It is *not* like "politics." No *s* at the end. The "rh" spelling comes from a silly affectation of certain scholars of ancient Greek, believing that the letter rho in Greek was mysteriously different from common *r*. It wasn't. So don't try to insert a breathiness into the *r*.

saLmon. No. Just "**sa**-mon." The *l* is silent. Yes, I know: English spelling, as I've already admitted, is insane. Its insanity comes from (1) the Great Vowel Shift in the 1400s (look it up) combined with (2) a decision that seems to have been made, even though the vowels did shift, to keep the historical spellings. Get used to it. After all, natives have to, as do French people writing French, which has similar historical spellings that now are silent. A curious advantage of such insanity, and one big reason rationalized spellings such as "thru" for *through* have not caught on, is that spelling does not therefore have to deal with different pronunciations in different dialects. Standard Italian is wholly phonetic in spelling, according to its base in

Tuscany. But that means that a Venetian or a Neapolitan has to pretend that the Tuscan spelling is how she talks too, though she doesn't when talking to Mamma.

"ar-**shi**-tekt" for "ar-ki-tekt": architect.

Key-**NES**-ian, that is "kay-NAYZ-ian." No. *Keynesian* is "KANES-ian." Three syllables, not four. Rhymes, as I said, with "brains." Or "walk without canes," which is good economic advice.

De**B**t. No. Just "det." The *b* is silent. Yes, I know. It's maddening.

Heir. No. It sounds the same as "air." The *h* is silent. Life is hard.

S**W**ord. No. Just "sord," though in 1400 it was pronounced with the *w*.

CONtribute or contri**BUTE**. You hear the first often in Britain. The American pronunciation is "con-TRIB-yute."

ans**W**er. No. "AN-sir." The *w* is silent. *Lasciate ogni speranza, voi ch'entrate inglese.*

PERsuade. No. The accent is on the second syllable: "per-SUADE."

Loan/borrow // teach/learn. Most languages seem not to have such distinctions. In English you loan to a friend, who is borrowing from you. You teach your students, who are learning from you. "Neither a borrower nor a lender be," said Polonius to Hamlet. Silly advice.

"Explain them X" should be "explain X **to** them." But "explain X" is fine if the people learning are not hanging around. "The professor explains latent factors." If you want to mention to whom he is explaining, you have to use "**to** the students."

"He accepted to" should be "he agreed to."

Nonnative speakers overuse and misuse the tense known to grammar as the continuative, because it is easier to remember. "My father is playing the piano" for "My father [habitually] plays the piano." The "is playing" says that he is *right now* playing it but might not be in the habit of doing so.

Languages drift, and it is hopeless to resist. A developing phrase in English among native speakers, for example, is "except for that" used in place of proper "except that." It makes no sense, but English speakers under age fifty in 2018 commonly use it, and by 2040 no one will be left who does not.

If You Didn't Stop Reading, Join the Flow

Good style is above all a matter of taste. Bad writers share with college sophomores, I noted at the outset, the conviction that matters of taste are "mere matters of opinion," the notion being that "opinion" is unarguable. A matter of taste, however, can be argued, often to a conclusion, about what the best rock music is, or the best movie, or the best ethics, or the best English style. The best social practice supports the conclusion, since that is what the best taste is. Many people with a plausible claim to know have listed rules for writing English, which fact is itself a powerful argument for learning good rules. Mark Twain listed seven, familiar to you now, which would revolutionize writing. The writer must

1. say what he is proposing to say, not merely come near it;
2. use the right word, not its second cousin;
3. eschew surplusage;
4. not omit necessary details;
5. avoid slovenliness of form;
6. use good grammar; and
7. employ a simple and straightforward style.

George Orwell, fifty years later, narrowed them down to six:

1. Never use a metaphor, simile, or other figure of speech which you are used to seeing in print.
2. Never use a long word where a short one will do.
3. If it is possible to cut a word out, always cut it out.
4. Never use the passive where you can use the active.
5. Never use a foreign phrase, a scientific word, or a jargon word if you can think of an everyday English equivalent.
6. Break any of these rules sooner than say anything outright barbarous.

To improve in writing you must become your own harshest editor and grader, as you must become your harshest coach to improve in running or your harshest critic to improve in thinking generally. If you don't often say to yourself, "Am I making sense? Am I speaking truth?" you will never learn to think for yourself. Good writing, which is a special form of critical thinking, is not effortless. Yet what is at first effortful becomes a happiness in the end, like any skill of civilization, an occasion for flow. You learned to play the guitar or to do gymnastics. You can learn to write skillfully.

In brief, then: We can do better, much better, than the say-what-you're-going-to-say, elegant variation, inefficient exposition, boilerplate, incoherent paragraphs, impenetrable tables, unemphatic word order, straggling sentences, contrived triplets, verbosity, nominalization, passive verbs, barbaric neologisms, abstractions, five-dollar words, teutonisms, acronyms, this-es, and fractured idioms of the worst modern prose.

Please, please, dears. For the grace and dignity of our lives, for the glory of our English tongue.

Scholars Talk Writing: Deirdre McCloskey

INTERVIEW BY RACHEL TOOR[1]
From *Chronicle of Higher Education*
March 20, 2016

Twenty years ago, Donald McCloskey, a brash and brilliant economist at the University of Iowa, surprised the academic world (and his family) by transitioning to Deirdre. In a 1996 profile in *The Chronicle*, McCloskey is quoted as saying, "I expected to lose my job. I was prepared to move to Spokane and become a secretary in a grain elevator, but I didn't have to."

No, she didn't. McCloskey has continued to thrive as a scholar. The final installment of her trilogy on the Bourgeois era, *Bourgeois Equality: How Ideas, Not Capital or Institutions, Enriched the World*, was published in May 2016 by the University of Chicago Press.

A few years ago, after an economist friend gave me a copy of McCloskey's wonderful style guide, *Economical Writing*, I wrote her a fan letter (from Spokane) and asked what kinds of changes had been made in the second edition of the guide, since the first was written by Donald and it was revised by Deirdre. She replied "Oh, it's mostly just moi!" It's a delightful little book, and I'm so pleased the University of Chicago Press is bringing out a third edition.

1. Originally published as Rachel Toor, "Scholars Talk Writing: Deirdre McCloskey," *Chronicle of Higher Education*, March 20, 2016, https://www.chronicle.com/article/Scholars-Talk-Writing-Deirdre /235767. Reprinted with permission from Toor and minor editorial changes.

McCloskey is the author of many books and articles including *Crossing: A Memoir*, a book about her transition that is at once breezy and profound. The same can often be said of her academic writing.

How were you able to escape the social scientist's disease of writing, well, badly? How did you learn to write well?

You know the standard is not high in economics. Whenever I get the slightest bit vain about my allegedly good writing, I open the *New Yorker* and weep. My family is filled with good writers, so I suppose there are a few genes involved. I am a stutterer, and I've noticed that stutters are often good writers: Churchill, Borges, Maugham, Updike, Lewis Carroll, Margaret Drabble, Philip Larkin. Stutterers avoid words that they think, or know, they will block on and therefore are good at finding another expression — which is to say that they develop large vocabularies and have a practiced sense of different ways of saying the same thing.

What is also true, as I tell my students, short of Borges — writing can be learned like any skill. We are not all as gifted as Edward Leamer is in econometrics, but we can learn the tricks if we study them. I got a head start with a teacher, Hal Melcher, at my boys' school in Cambridge (now coed and called Buckingham Browne & Nichols: lots of funny stories there). In college one had to write a lot, and I was smart-aleck good at it. But when I got to graduate school, I found my style deteriorating because I had to combine good style with *truth*. Oy. I couldn't just *write*.

The recovery took decades — attending steadily to books on style such as, of course, Strunk and White, on which my own little book is modeled, but then, among many others, *The Reader over Your Shoulder* (I was struck by the dissection there by Robert Graves and Alan Hodge of a passage from Keynes, who is much admired in economics for his style), and Joseph M. Williams's *Style: Ten Lessons in Clarity and Grace*, and Richard A. Lanham's *Revising Prose*.

I accumulated rules and rules and rules, probably a few score of them. As Dick Lanham says, it's revising that does it, and at that point you can be guided by The Rules. I use The Rules every time I write: express parallel ideas in parallel form, don't indulge in elegant variation, allow only one element of a sentence to get long, and on and on and on. Double oy.

And I noted how the best writers in economics did it: Robert Solow, for example, who lets his personality through. I had the advantage over many economists of reading outside of economics: Willa Cather, A. N. Wilson, Martha Nussbaum, Richard Rorty, Howard Becker, and Wayne Booth. (Wayne was delighted when I confirmed to him that I had written that "When I grow up I want to be a female Wayne Booth.")

Given the many differences you point out in Crossing *about how Donald and Deirdre think, felt, and interacted in the world, surely there were changes in your prose style when you transitioned. Can you say something about gender and writing, and how your crossing affected your prose?*

I do not want to be accused of essentialism. But as a first- and third-wave feminist (not second wave — e.g., the startlingly transphobe Germaine Greer), I note differences. It's hard for me to judge, true, because when I read my earlier stuff I'm reading it philosophically for the argument, not rhetorically for the style. The big item I reckon is the style of *argument*. I still write always with an argument, which might sound male — unless you met my mother, from whom I learned how to argue! But the arguing is less relentless now, more diffident, as arguments should be if you are interested in the actual truth and want to establish it together with your reader.

As a young man I was proud of *crushing* an opponent in my writing — as though on my high school football team (of which, by the way, I was cocaptain). Now I am trying to make common cause with the reader, and trying also to be truthfully gentle with the "opponents." It came naturally — not as Rule No. 15 in How to Be a Woman. My joke, though, is that I can't tell whether any improvement is because I became a woman (within the limits, alas, of biology and life history) . . . or because I finally grew up.

It's interesting that one of your fears as a transperson, at least early on, was of being "read." A question I often find myself asking as I read a piece of prose is "What is this writer afraid of?" I think much writing — especially by academics — goes wrong due, simply, to fear. Much bad prose is the result of being afraid of not being or seeming smart enough, or not knowing enough.

So true. As C. Wright Mills put it, we won't recover from the academic prose until we recover from the academic *pose*. The advantage of being a woman and being older is that you are licensed to quit the young, male posturing and just say what you've discovered. Write what you have to say, openhandedly.

But the trouble is that a young scholar does have to establish "ethos," as the Greeks said. The older professor then gets stuck in pomposity, fearful he'll be found out. I teach business subjects each summer to European doctoral students — formerly in France and now Greece (it's cheaper) — and try to get them to get over the fears. But even without fully overcoming their fears, the tricks I can teach them are often enough to raise the level of their prose. For example, leave off anticipating ("This paper is organized as follows").

Can you talk about your revising?

I reread obsessively, cold, following the Graves and Hodge technique of stopping when I can't follow it or I see an infelicity. The advantage of word processing is that revision is easy. The disadvantage is the temptation to preserve one's golden prose even when it's actually a brick. Waiting long enough so that you see your prose as foreign helps. My books have got longer since word processing.

Another trick is to read your own draft immediately after reading someone else's excellent writing. I dote on Richard Rorty, for example, and find myself imitating his tic of starting sentences with "We bourgeois liberals," inviting the reader to adopt his line. If I read Jane Austen, as I often do, I find myself using comical little ironies set into the last word in the sentence, most famously in "It is a truth universally acknowledged, that a single man in possession of a good fortune must be in want of a wife." It is good to read your own work with good prose ringing in your ears. After all, there's enough bad prose ringing too. Get the right ring.

Who reads or edits your early drafts?

I do. True, I let the brilliant copyeditors whom the University of Chicago Press hires give me two or three great suggestions on each page, and I get the credit! I've gradually realized, by the way, that the sort of detailed copyediting I do on other people's writing isn't effective rhetorically. It doesn't much help the person you are trying to help, if they are the types who resist being edited. Eventually I acquired the professional attitude about it—namely, if a good writer and editor like Carol Fisher Saller (of *The Subversive Copy Editor*) tells me something is wrong, it is (Carol once detected a *mathematical* error in an economic argument I was running).

Sitting down with students and going slowly over a paragraph, word by word, does help. But it's hard for students (and for too many senior professors) to take the attitude—which daily journalists learn the hard way—that the (competent, tasteful) editor knows best. I have run a decades-long attempt to get a friend, a brilliant scholar and a fine writer (even though English is not his native language), to give up that seventh-grade ornament of bad prose "not only . . . but also." He resists yet.

You've been involved in a number of writing workshops, including one at George Mason University. What are such workshops like?

They are my idea of academic heaven, which I have repeatedly tried to reproduce after first experiencing it in Alexander Gerschenkron's economic history workshop at Harvard in the 1960s. It's how I teach advanced graduate students: I miss it so much that I just started a class (having retired from giving classes for pay) that meets every Sunday night for a meal and workshopping. Huzzah!

The key is to love your colleagues. You have to be together long enough to get over the academic pose ("Heh, I'm the expert here") and learn to listen. Love is important, and often overlooked. Love makes it possible for the writer whose work is being tested to accept criticism gracefully, since she knows it is meant in love. Men don't grasp it, usually. They are so busy competing that they don't realize that what actually works is cooperation. Whoops — sorry: Gender Candor Alert.

At the University of Iowa in the Project on Rhetoric of Inquiry (*poroi*: Greek for "river fords" and "ways and means"; I cofounded it in the early 1980s), we had, and have, a rule that you could not just a present a paper. You had ten minutes at the outset of a presentation to add what you wanted on the spot, and then the discussion of the paper started. That meant that most of the audience had to read the paper beforehand. More usually in academic presentations, no one reads the paper beforehand because the audience knows the paper will be presented — in some fields, actually read aloud. And so the author filibusters for most of the time, and then there's only a few minutes of discussion. That approach is pointless for the job of workshopping — that is, helping the author to improve the paper.

What are your weaknesses as a writer?

Prolixity, I am told. The criticism annoys me because I don't see length as a problem if each sentence and each paragraph is worth the candle. Look at the philosopher Charles Taylor, who writes very long books, each sentence of which deserves to be engraved in stone. On the other hand, the reader is always right ("Give the lady what she wants"). Also, my writing has too many references and too many levels of sophistication (look at my quotation just now of the great department store magnate Marshall Field of Chicago).

When I was a junior professor at the University of Chicago the great historian William McNeill praised a piece of mine for its breadth of reference, and I'm afraid the praise went to my head. Bill doesn't write that way. I suspect he was trying to alert me in his gentlemanly way to a fault. But many good writers do write in a complicated if charming and intelligent way — Clifford Geertz, for example. So it's hopeless.

House Rules: Teaching Materials

I taught writing in every course I gave, whether in economics or history or whatever. Here's a slice of the handouts for the teaching.

In series use a comma before the *and*: X, Y, and Z.
The trouble is that without it the reader finds
it easy to think you mean "X and another thing
combining Y and Z."

Two spaces after a period, one after a comma.
Repeat after me: Two spaces after . . . It's the old
convention of typewriters and is easier to read.

Get the word *stated* out of your active vocabularies.
"The book stated" is a childish way of saying
"Coffin et al. claim."

Don't use *they* as singular to avoid a choice of *he* or
she; often enough you are not even in *that* bind:
"In order for a business to prosper they need to
find a market" should of course be "it": "In order
for a business to prosper it needs to find a market."
When you do have a he/she problem, pick one and
go with it.

Relative pronoun (*that*) **for people is *who* or *whom*.**
"If one is known to someone who [not "that"]
works for the FBI . . ."

It is not entirely uncontroversial, but no comma is
needed after an initial phrase such as "Considering
the options **[no comma here, despite what
your teacher in 8th grade told you!]** the B
choice is best." Or "In summary **[no comma]** the

Enlightenment blah, blah." Sometimes — rarely — the comma will be useful if otherwise the sentence would be confusing. But this will almost never be the case if the next phrase starts with *the* or *this*. (See the example at the end of the next item.)

Get "I believe" and "I think" out of your writing. Putting yourself into the writing — using *I* — is fine *if your opinion is the point*. When it's not, keep yourself out of the picture. As Strunk and White say, "To deliver unsolicited opinions is to suggest that the demand for them is brisk." To put it another way, you are being asked for *facts* and *arguments*, put into a good *style*, not opinions.

Citations in the author/page style are fine, but do the punctuation correctly. The period goes *outside* the citation: "is ten to one (Jacobsen, 282)." Not "is ten to one. Jacobsen, 282" with no period at all after the parentheses.

Always staple papers. Little carelessnesses like turning in two sheets with the corners folded, fourth-grade style, get your reader off to a bad start. Imagine that reader as your boss. She'll fire you, believe me.

TOP TEN SIGNS THAT SOME PEOPLE ARE NOT PAYING ATTENTION TO AUNT DEIRDRE'S GOOD ADVICE ON DEVELOPING A GROWNUP WRITING STYLE

10. Using *the fact that* or *due to*
9. Using *the former* or *the latter*
8. Using *this* or *these* too much when *the* or *such a* would do
7. Not spellchecking
6. Not double spacing

5. Not getting the citation punctuation right
4. Not inserting that second comma in A, B, and C
3. Still thinking that a semicolon is the same as a colon
2. Still, using, too, many, commas,,,,,,,,,,,,,,,
   AND THE TOP SIGN THAT etc., etc.:
1.) STILL NOT USING TWO SPACES AFTER A FINAL STOP (period, exclamation point, question mark)

ADD THIS TO YOUR HANDOUTS ON STYLE

- "Buzz, buzz" (Diamond 2019, 30). Note where the period goes: *after* the citation.
- No need for ellipses before and after a quotation: ". . . buzz, buzz . . ." (Diamond, 30) is wrong.
- A, B, and C. X, Y, or X. **Note the comma before "and" and "or."** (And note where I put the period in that last sentence: inside the quote marks—odd though it seems, that's the printing convention.
- No title pages. No padding.
- No "In my opinion" (computer folks say "IMHO"). The women especially need to watch this. It's a good and sensible thing to do in conversation, this self-deprecation. It's fatal to an argument in prose.

If we circle something there's something wrong with it—bad choice of word, or using a word contrary to the Holy Writ of *Economical Writing*.

ANOTHER TEN SIGNS THAT SOMEONE IS NOT READING THAT BRILLIANT BOOK BY DEIRDRE MCCLOSKEY, *ECONOMICAL WRITING*

1. Using commas religiously after introductory clauses

2. "this . . . . this . . . . this"
3. Starting sentences with "However,"
4. Using the word *process*
5. Using *not only . . . but also*
6. Not grasping the difference between a colon (:) and a semicolon (;)
7. Not reading out loud: silliness, rhymes, etc.
8. No marks on the paper: no last proofreading
9. Not using two spaces after a period or ! or ?
10. Full justification

ONCE AGAIN, CLASS

Any paper without two spaces after a full stop → one grade off! [We'll start applying this later in the term.]

A check mark, you know, means "Hmm. Good point!"

Note *this/those/these* and if there seem to be too many, knock 'em out! Use *the*, or sometimes *such*.

Avoid clichés — that is, set phrases you are accustomed to hearing: they give an impression of not thinking. "Jack up the prices" (not economics anyway).

That introductory comma is usually *not* necessary, whatever Ms. Jones said. Put in commas *by ear*. And always: "A, B, and C."

Pay attention to my tips on The Right Word: if I've suggested another, it's because you've misused the word; learn not to by paying attention.

People take *who*, not *that* or *which*: "The people *who* we saw," not "The people *that* we saw."

No *due to* and other Bad Phrases (see the book).

"Note the order of punctuation in quotations." (I've been watching it recently in books and newspapers, by the way, and notice that copyeditors sometimes get it wrong.)

Get yourself and your opinions out of the pieces.
Your boss wants to know what you think, but
not hedged around with "I think." When you are
talking about *I* you aren't talking about the subject,
are you?

Always indent the first line of paragraphs (if you
learned to write abroad you might not know this).

Learn the different between (:) and (;). It's this: when
B *follows from* or *illustrates* A, then use a colon (:),
as I just did; when B is *parallel or similar to* A, use
a semicolon (;), as I just did.

Don't repeat. Ask yourself: Am I just filling in here?

What do you put at the end of a question, always?
How do you know that the sentence is a question?
Does tone of voice tell you? Are you getting tired of
my little joke?

Note spellings: *elsewhere*, not *else where*. *Don't*, not
Do n't (extra space).

Don't start sentences with _____ [you fill it in!]
instead of *But*.

Do feel free to start sentences with *And* or *But*.

Due to the fact that is an idiotic and unlovely phrase.
Or *Because of the fact that*. Please. Ditto *not
only . . . but also. As well as* (usually).

You don't need to keep reminding us that you are
talking about, say, the textbook, or the nineteenth
century.

Don't be afraid of being funny, if you can pull it off.
Let's see some *Saturday Night Live* humor.

Never *and/or* or *he/she*.

Cliché: *right place at the right time*.

Like in → *As in*.

Things, such as the economy, "going up" are not
economic ways of talking.

Avoid the Dread Comma Splice, it is the fault of merely adding on a sentence connected with a comma, you can see here what the problem is, it is hard to read, some great writers do it, by the way.

If you read what you've written out loud you will correct many infelicities (= unhappy turns of phrase).

To test whether you are getting these such points, try this.

Quiz on *Economical Writing*

1. "The President went to see the Chinese premier, so that the Chief Executive could discuss the Korean situation with the Chinese leader." What's wrong? *Name it.*

2. Correct the following: < *Landes thinks "Europe is neat". (Landes, p. 467)* >

3. What infelicity do both these sentences make? Mark it.

   During the 19th century, the United Kingdom included Great Britain and Ireland.

   Unfortunately, Landes is Eurocentric.

4. How about this one: "England, Scotland and little Wales make up the island of 'Great Britain'."

5. This paragraph has a problem. This author doesn't even notice that she has this problem. This problem is the pointless overuse of a certain word. This word is being used essentially as a substitute for *the* — which we already have in English. Circle this problem word in this paragraph.

6. "Not only is using the phrase *due to* unnecessarily fancy, but it also is a sign of childish writing." Comment?

7. The writer of this brief paragraph does not understand a tiny little convention in typing. Missing it makes her prose hard to read. The ends of sentences are not clear, and the prose therefore blurs. What is her mistake? Did she just make it also in the previous sentence? *When will she learn?!*

8. The process of the process of writing is a difficult process. This process of rewriting is important in the process. The key to this process is to eliminate needless words. What word does Professor McCloskey have in mind in this process? *Rewrite the paragraph making the necessary correction.*

APPENDIX
Applying *Economical Writing* to Become Your Own Best Editor

STEPHEN T. ZILIAK

Professors demand good writing, and students are told to supply it. But how? In the modern academy a professor's attention is stretched in many different directions, and increasingly large class sizes don't help. Meantime students are given too little advice on how to write, and the advice they do get is often vague and, though well-intentioned, almost useless. A dancer or surgeon or classical musician is not much helped by being told "This is a rough transition" or "Punctuation is wrong." Writers either. Students require something more.

In the early 2000s I was teaching large classes at the Georgia Institute of Technology when I invented the McZ♯ method of writing and rewriting using the numbered chapters and their underlying principles in *Economical Writing*. The McZ♯ method (as in **Mc**Closkey**Z**iliak; say "Mick-ZEE-number") has proven to be a fast, effective, and efficient way to teach, write, edit, and rewrite good prose. How I came upon the idea will not surprise economists: scarcity is the mother of invention, and invention is the writer's greatest resource. Like most teachers, I wanted to give good and useful comments on student papers, but my own research projects and other duties constrained me. The poet's dream of writing out brilliant sentence-length comments in the margins of every paper — paper by paper, line by line — was just that: a recurring dream which couldn't be fulfilled under current constraints. One day, while facing a pile of ungraded papers, I found a solution.

Here is a step-by-step guide for applying the principles in *Economical Writing* using the McZ# method. The method has been tested and proved by me and McCloskey and others at all levels of instruction, from freshman seminar to postdoc workshop, at numerous universities in the United States and Europe. The description here assumes you are a student writer in a classroom setting, with an instructor who is already familiar with the book and the McZ# method. But much of the method is self-guided and could apply if you are a writer working on your own or with an editor, a peer, or any other second pair of eyes. In any setting, it will help turn poor writers into good and good writers into great.

1. Quickly read *Economical Writing* all the way through, taking in as much of the feel and advice of McCloskey's little book as you can but focusing at first on the "feel" — her voice, her playfulness, her learnedness, her earnestness, and her commitment to complete the job (time: about 1 hour). Notice how she is speaking to *you.*

2. Then read the book a second time. Slow down and carefully examine a small selection of chapters, those you believe could help you the most right now. Begin to memorize chapter titles according to the *action* that is to be taken from them, especially from chapter 8 (write early, not late) to chapter 35 (the Twain and Orwell rules). Abbreviate chapter numbers and titles: for example, McZ 12 = "Avoid Boilerplate" and McZ 30 = "Avoid *This, That, These,* and *Those*" (time: about 1 more hour).

3. Write a first draft of your paper, keeping the McZ#s in mind as you write. The McZ# method works on any manuscript length, but it's best to start with something short. Before you write ten or twelve pages, paragraph one needs to pass the McZ# test.

4. Print a copy of your draft. Alternatively, your instructor might ask you to use the Comment function to mark up the document electronically. (I prefer paper, but that's just me. I also like vintage bikes, bow ties, and music of the Baroque.)

5. Read your paper word by word and line by line. Circle each word, passage, or punctuation mark that is in violation of one or more McZ# rules. Note in a side margin or between two lines the relevant number: "McZ 13" if you're not controlling your tone; "McZ 30" every time you find a *this*, *that, these, those* or similar vague placeholder, which will be often. And so on, through "McZ 35: Twain's rules and Orwell's rules." McZ 35, Orwell #1 and Twain #1–2 are especially important for the ethical economist.

6. Find and note a total of at least four McZ#s for each page of your paper. (If all you manage to circle is *this* or *that*, marking "McZ 30," you are cheating the system: try again.) A five-page paper should have around twenty circled and noted areas.

7. Submit your marked-up paper.

8. Your instructor will find additional McZ#s and will offer tips on how to fix the McZ# violations noted. For example, to fix McZ 30, she might suggest that you see McZ 27 (be concrete, which means writing

with images, not vague placeholders: *bread* and *beer* and *democracy*, not *consumables* and *liquids* and *governmental structures*). If your paragraph does not have a point (McZ 14) you can fix it with McZ 35, Twain #1 (say what you intend to say; don't merely come close) and Orwell #1 (avoid popular metaphors and other figures of speech you are used to seeing in print).

9. Once your paper is returned to you, revise and resubmit it. Make every editorial change suggested. Reread the new version with a cold eye, and make any other adjustments keeping the McZ#s in mind. Print your revised paper and submit both marked-up copies, each clearly identified.

10. Sometimes the result is not good enough, and one more cycle of the McZ# method is needed. Some of you may complain, "But my paper is finished: why do I have to put more marks on it?" To which McCloskey and I join Hemingway in replying, "No, your paper is not finished — not that kind of finished."

A couple more tools. One way to solve that "I feel stuck" problem caused by excessive boilerplate (McZ 12), vague word usage (McZ 27), and other bad word choices (McZ 26) is to employ what I call the *image-to-sound ratio*. If a sentence sounds like Charlie Brown's teacher *blah-blah-blahing* into a landscape with more clouds than Ireland, you'll want a fix. The image-to-sound ratio delivers exactly what it says: it's a numeric ratio that counts up the total number of concrete images used in a sentence (Charlie Brown, clouds, Ireland) and divides that number by the total number of sounds uttered. Try it out. Take a random sentence from your paper. If the image-to-sound ratio falls far below 40 percent, you're probably speaking in bureaucratic or other boilerplate terms, like Charlie Brown's teacher, such as by overusing vague or cliché filler words (McZ 12, 26, 35, Orwell #1). On the opposite side of the scale, if your image-to-sound ratio is high, near 100 percent, you ought to take up poetry or song writing, and probably already have! To up your image-to-sound ratio, replace deadweight loss with concrete imagery. Words such as *however, nonetheless,* and *interesting* are not themselves interesting, however, and should be dropped or replaced nonetheless.

Writing haiku, another tool of economical writing, can help. Economical writing is the art of allocating scarce rhetorical means to a number of noneconomic ends. The most efficient form of economical writing is instanced by classical Japanese haiku writing after Bashō (Ziliak 2009). I call it "haiku economics." Haiku economics is economical writing par excellence, and a second tool to employ when you are feeling "stuck."

Conventionally consisting of seventeen sound counts arranged on three lines of 5-7-5, the haiku form can tell a vivid, imagistic story—having an introduction, a middle, and a conclusion—despite the charmingly tight budget constraint. A three-act haiku play, so to speak, in seventeen syllables, can gain more substantive ground than many hundreds of sounds made by boilerplate economics. In more than twenty years of teaching I've found that economical writing tends to improve with increased attention to the rules and attitudes of medieval haiku poets (Ziliak 2011).

Turning a poorly written sentence into a haiku can win you more than increased clarity and coherence. Compare a single haiku by Bashō with three sequential sentences written recently by a representative economist at the Na-

tional Bureau of Economic Research (add up the McZ#
violations; in the next three sentences we find at least
eleven!)

University Economist
If these households also make other investments
in their health, failing to account for them biases
estimates of the effects of pollution. To address this,
economists have employed a wide range of quasi-
experimental techniques to provide causal estimates
of the effect of pollution on health and human capital.
Second, stemming from this optimizing framework,
economists have placed a considerable focus on
avoidance behavior. (https://www.nber.org/reporter
/2017number2/neidell.html)

Haiku Economist
The young farm-child
interrupts rice husking to
gaze up at the moon
(Bashō, quoted in Ziliak 2009)

The McZ# method and related tools will help you become your own best editor. That's what we seek, after
all — "education as the practice of freedom," in bell hooks's
memorable phrase. The McZ# method is fast and efficient.
Economical editing for economical writing. Win, win.

References

Barzun, Jacques. 2001. *Simple and Direct: A Rhetoric for Writers* 4th ed. New York: Harper and Row.

Barzun, Jacques, and Henry F. Graff. (1970) 2003. *The Modern Researcher.* New York: Harcourt Brace.

Becker, Howard S. 2007. *Writing for Social Scientists: How to Start and Finish Your Thesis, Book, or Article.* 2nd ed. Chicago: University of Chicago Press.

Blundell, William E. 1988. *The Art and Craft of Feature Writing.* New York: Plume.

Booth, Wayne C. 1974. *Modern Dogma and the Rhetoric of Assent.* Chicago: University of Chicago Press.

Booth, Wayne C., Gregory G. Colomb, Joseph M. Williams, Joseph Bizup, and William T. FitzGerald. 2016. *The Craft of Research.* 4th ed. Chicago: University of Chicago Press.

Bowersock, Glen W. 1983/1984. "The Art of the Footnote." *American Scholar* 53:54–63.

Brodkey, Linda. 1994. "Writing on the Bias." *College English* 56 (September): 527–47.

Csikszentmihalyi, Mihaly. 1997. *Finding Flow: The Psychology of Engagement with Everyday Life.* New York: Basic.

Diamond, Arthur M., Jr., and David M. Levy. 1991. "Stylometrics: Statistical Evidence on the Decline in the Clarity of Writing in the Economics Profession." Paper presented at the annual meeting of the Society for Social Studies of Science, Boston, November 12.

Dillard, Annie. 1989. *The Writing Life.* New York: Harper.

Fish, Stanley. 2001. *How Milton Works.* Cambridge, MA: Harvard University Press.

Fowler, H. W. (1926) 1965. *Modern English Usage.* 2nd ed. Rev. Ernest Gowers. Oxford: Oxford University Press.

Galbraith, J. K. 1978. "Writing, Typing and Economics." *Atlantic* 241 (March): 102–5.

Gardner, John. 1983. *The Art of Fiction: Notes on Craft for Young Writers.* New York: Alfred A. Knopf.

Gowers, Ernest. 1962. *The Complete Plain Words*. London: Penguin. (Also subsequent eds.)

Graff, Gerald, and Cathy Birkenstein. (2006) 2014. *They Say, I Say: The Moves That Matter in Academic Writing*. 2nd ed. New York: W. W. Norton.

Graves, Robert, and Alan Hodge. (1943) 1961. *The Reader over Your Shoulder: A Handbook for Writers of English Prose*. New York: Macmillan.

Hall, Donald. 1979. *Writing Well*. 3rd ed. Boston: Little, Brown.

Halmos, Paul R. (1973) 1981. In *How to Write Mathematics*, edited by Norman E. Steenrod et al., 19–48. N.p.: American Mathematics Society.

Hanawalt, Barbara A. 1979. *Crime and Conflict in English Communities, 1300–1348*. Cambridge, MA: Harvard University Press.

Hayek, Friedrich. 1994. *Hayek on Hayek*. Interviews and essays edited by Stephen Kresge and Leif Wener. Chicago: University of Chicago Press.

Lanham, Richard A. 2006. *Revising Business Prose*. 5th ed. New York: Pearson.

Lanham, Richard A. 2007. *Revising Prose*. 5th ed. New York: Macmillan.

Lucas, F. L. (1955) 2012. *Style*. London: Cassell.

Machlup, Fritz. (1963) 1967. *Essays in Economic Semantics*. New York: Norton.

McCloskey, Deirdre Nansen. 1985. "Economical Writing." *Economic Inquiry* 24 (April): 187–222.

McCloskey, Deirdre Nansen. 1992. "Writing as a Responsibility of Science: A Reply to Laband and Taylor." *Economic Inquiry* 30 (October): 689–95.

McCloskey, Deirdre Nansen. 1998. *The Rhetoric of Economics*. 2nd rev. ed. Madison: University of Wisconsin Press.

McCloskey, Deirdre Nansen, and Stephen T. Ziliak. 1996. "The Standard Error of Regressions." *Journal of Economic Literature* 34 (March): 97–114.

Medawar, Peter. 1964. "Is the Scientific Paper Fraudulent?" *Saturday Review* 47 (August 1): 42–43.

Mills, C. Wright. 1959. "On Intellectual Craftsmanship." In *The Sociological Imagination*. New York: Grove.

Morgenstern, Oskar. 1963. *On the Accuracy of Economic Observations*. 2nd ed. Princeton, NJ: Princeton University Press.

Mueller, John. 1989. *Retreat from Doomsday: The Obsolescence of Major War.* New York: Basic Books.

Oakeshott, Michael. 1933. "Poetry as a Voice in the Conversation of Mankind." In *Experience and Its Modes*; reprinted in *Rationalism in Politics* (1962). New York: Basic Books.

Orwell, George. (1946) 1968. "Politics and the English Language." In *The Collected Essays, Journalism and Letters of George Orwell*, vol. 4, *In Front of Your Nose, 1945–1950*, edited by Sonia Orwell and Ian Argus. New York: Harcourt Brace Jovanovich.

Piaget, Jean, and Jean-Claude Bringuier. 1980. *Conversations with Jean Piaget.* Chicago: University of Chicago Press.

Pinker, Steven. 2011. *The Better Angels of Our Nature: Why Violence Has Declined.* New York: Viking Books.

Popper, Karl. 1976. *Unended Quest: An Intellectual Autobiography.* Glasgow: Collins.

Quintilian. 1980. *Institutio oratoria.* Cambridge, MA: Harvard University Press.

Salant, Walter. 1969. "Writing and Reading in Economics." *Journal of Political Economy* 77 (July/August): 545–58.

Sartre, Jean Paul. 1948. *Anti-Semite and Jew* [*Réflexions sur la question juive*, 1945]. Translated by J. Becker. New York: Schocken Books.

Sellar, W. C., and R. J. Yeatman. 1930. *1066 and All That.* London: Methuen.

Smith, Adam. (1759–90) 1976–82. *The Theory of Moral Sentiments.* Glasgow edition. Edited by D. D. Raphael and A. L. Macfie. Indianapolis: Liberty Classics.

Solow, Robert. 1981. "Does Economics Make Progress?" *Bulletin of the American Academy of Arts and Sciences* 26 (December): 11–31.

Strunk, William, Jr., and E. B. White. 1979. *The Elements of Style.* 3rd ed. New York: Macmillan. (Also subsequent eds.)

Thomas, Francis-Noel, and Mark Turner. 2011. *Clear and Simple as the Truth: Writing Classic Prose.* 2nd ed. Princeton, NJ: Princeton University Press.

Tufte, Edward R. 1983. *The Visual Display of Quantitative Information.* Cheshire, CT: Graphics Press.

Tufte, Edward R. 1990. *Envisioning Information.* Cheshire, CT: Graphics Press.

Tufte, Edward R. 2003. "Power Point Is Evil." *Wired*, September 1.

Twain, Mark. 1895. "Fenimore Cooper's Literary Offenses." *North American Review*, July. Reprinted in *The Unabridged Mark Twain*. Philadelphia: Running Press, 1976.

Ulam, Stanislaw. 1976. *Adventures of a Mathematician*. New York: Scribner's.

Webster's New World Dictionary of the American Language. 2nd college ed. 1976. Cleveland: William Collins & World.

Williams, Joseph M. (1981) 2016. *Style: Lessons in Clarity and Grace*. Glenview, IL: Scott, Foresman.

Williamson, Samuel T. 1947. "How to Write like a Social Scientist." *Saturday Review* 20 (October).

Ziliak, Stephen T. 2009. "Haiku Economics: Little Teaching Aids for Big Economic Pluralists." *International Journal of Pluralism and Economics Education* 1, nos. 1/2: 108–29.

Ziliak, Stephen T. 2011. "Haiku Economics: Money, Metaphor, and the Invisible Hand." *Poetry* 197, no. 5 (January): 314–16. Repr. 2017 in *Who Reads Poetry? Fifty Views from "Poetry" Magazine*, edited by Fred Sasaki and Don Share. Chicago: University of Chicago Press.

Index

Books by Deirdre Nansen McCloskey

(* University of Chicago Press books)

Economic Maturity and Entrepreneurial Decline: British Iron and Steel, 1870–1913

Enterprise and Trade in Victorian Britain: Essays in Historical Economics

The Applied Theory of Price, 2nd ed.

The Rhetoric of Economics, 2nd ed.

Econometric History

*If You're So Smart: The Narrative of Economic Expertise

Knowledge and Persuasion in Economics

The Vices of Economists; The Virtues of the Bourgeoisie

*Crossing: A Memoir

(edited by Stephen T. Ziliak) *Measurement and Meaning in Economics: The Essential Deirdre McCloskey*

How to Be an Economist* *Though Human

*The Secret Sins of Economics

*The Bourgeois Virtues: Ethics for an Age of Commerce

(with Stephen T. Ziliak) *The Cult of Statistical Significance: How the Standard Error Costs Us Jobs, Justice, and Lives*

*Bourgeois Dignity: Why Economics Can't Explain the Modern World

*Bourgeois Equality: How Ideas, N Capital or Institutions, Enriched the World

Why Liberalism? Essays for a New Liberalism